THE
FLOWER
CHEF

THE FLOWER CHEF

A MODERN GUIDE TO DO-IT-YOURSELF FLORAL ARRANGEMENTS

CARLY CYLINDER

EDITED BY AMARA HOLSTEIN

GRAND CENTRAL
Life & Style

NEW YORK   BOSTON

Grand Central Life & Style
Hachette Book Group
1290 Avenue of the Americas
New York, NY 10104
GrandCentralLifeandStyle.com

First Edition: March 2016

Grand Central Life & Style is an imprint of Grand Central Publishing. The Grand Central Life & Style name and logo are trademarks of Hachette Book Group, Inc.

The Hachette Speakers Bureau provides a wide range of authors for speaking events. To find out more, go to www.HachetteSpeakersBureau.com or call (866) 376-6591.

The publisher is not responsible for websites (or their content) that are not owned by the publisher.

Print book interior design by Amy Sly

Library of Congress Cataloging-in-Publication Data has been applied for.
ISBNs: 978-1-4555-5549-9 (hardcover), 978-1-4555-5550-5 (ebook)

10 9 8 7 6 5 4 3 2

Printed in the United States of America

Q-MA

TO MY DAD, LARRY, AND MY MOM, LAUREN. THANK YOU FOR INSTILLING INDEPENDENCE, CONFIDENCE, AND ORIGINALITY IN ME FROM A YOUNG AGE. AND TO MY BROTHER, MATTHEW. I LOVE YOU AS ONLY A BIG SISTER CAN.

116

163

200

9

90

207

CONTENTS

Introduction **8**

INTRODUCTION

People often say to me, "Oh, you must always have *loved* flowers! Your passion is so contagious!" The truth is, owning a flower business—not to mention regularly teaching classes, creating floral content for brands, and writing this floral design book—is actually the *last* thing I thought I'd be doing. Only after a series of chance happenings on a path full of twists, turns, and stoplights did I discover my life's true passion.

Before I moved to LA at age nineteen and took a job at a florist, my knowledge of flowers was limited to carnations and roses. My first week on the job, I misspelled *orchid* as *orchard* and in return received a look from the manager that could've frozen water. I couldn't figure out how to make a wrapped bouquet until an associate showed me how to put the tissue paper between two layers of cellophane so that the paper didn't get soaked, simple as that. But despite my early mishaps, I loved being surrounded by flowers and I loved watching the creativity and artistry of the floral designers.

I began to carefully watch the designers at the floral shop where I worked, and then I'd experiment with flower design when I got home. I discovered that using your hands to create a work of art out of nature is a fun, fulfilling sensory experience. I still savor the way a knife slices through wet, dense floral foam and the crisp sound of roses getting a fresh cut. I adore walking into a room and breathing in the luscious scent of beautifully arranged blooms. The fragrance opens my senses, awakens my mind, and calms my being.

It had always been a dream of mine to open a business, and when I discovered my passion for flowers, I knew the business I wanted to start. It was toward the end of 2009, at the urging of my best friend and roommate, that I decided to go ahead and start a floral business right out of my quaint apartment in the South Bay area of Los Angeles.

And so my flower business was born.

I called it Flour, with the intention of eventually turning it into a combined café and florist. I started experimenting with floral design using inexpensive flowers that I could get nearby. My brother built me a website, and I began filling it with photographs of my original designs. I vividly remember freaking out when I got my first order on the website: *Someone is paying me to arrange flowers for them! I don't know what I'm doing!* But I swallowed my fear and got to work.

During those first few years, I hustled. I was aggressive about getting myself out there. I cold-called potential clients, attended networking events, and did lots of media outreach. Slowly but surely, business picked up and my design skills improved. I was able to rent a space at a wholesale florist where I oversaw a team of designers for weddings and events.

Now Flour LA, Inc., is a thriving bicoastal floral design business. As an entrepreneur and a self-taught florist, I make my own rules. My designs are inspired by fashion, art, nature, and whatever else catches my fancy.

With this book, my goal is to teach you everything I know—how to buy flowers, how to care for them, how to arrange them—I mean *everything*. I'm here to make floral design easy and accessible. I want to teach you the fundamental techniques, to inspire you to get creative and to make your own designs. And I want to show you how to make beautiful and original arrangements out of everyday flowers.

This book is for everyone: for people who have never worked with flowers and are looking to discover a new creative outlet; for the crafters, the DIYers, and the admirers of flowers who've always had a deep interest and desire to learn; and for those in the lifestyle industry who want to incorporate floral design into their work. I also hope it will serve as a valuable resource for individuals already working in the design field who want to expand and update their techniques.

I wrote this for you—the novice, the dreamer, the professional, the artist. My heart and soul went into this book and I hope it will inform, instruct, and inspire.

With love and gratitude,

Carly Cylinder

1

HOW TO USE THIS BOOK

As a child, I would watch Julia Child on reruns of *The French Chef*, drawn to her upbeat personality and her easygoing teaching style. She helped novices and professionals alike learn advanced cooking techniques—making fine cuisine both fun and accessible. So when I considered writing a book, I thought about Julia Child, along with the current crop of TV chefs who teach basic skills to home cooks, and I realized that there was no one doing the same thing in the floral design world. I wanted to be that person.

This is the book I needed when I was starting out. No fancy scientific terms, no rare flowers, no convoluted handmade drawings. Each arrangement is written like a recipe with an ingredient list and step-by-step instructions that are clear and easy to follow. This is the book you'll keep in your kitchen next to your favorite cookbooks—simply pick out some flowers at the farmers' market that strike your fancy, come home, flip through this book, and whip up a beautiful arrangement in no time flat.

Every arrangement was chosen to demonstrate a specific method or technique, but feel free to mix and match techniques and arrangements. Many of the techniques I use are traditional and widely practiced. Many others, however, I made up myself. If there's one thing I hope to accomplish with this book, it's to inspire you to experiment and create your own designs. Flower arranging should be fun, and I hope this book will give you the tools you need to come up with your own unique designs.

Most of all, think of this like a cook book rather than a baking book. In other words, feel free to improvise—the ingredients and measurements aren't absolute. If a recipe calls for one rose, but the one you have is puny, just add two or three more to make up the difference in size. Or maybe your ti leaf is too big, so you trim it down a little. Flower arranging doesn't have to be absolutely precise. Add a dash more spice here or substitute an ingredient there to get your own perfectly blended floral dish. Take what I'm saying as a guide and use this book as a springboard for your own creativity.

HOW TO READ
THE RECIPES

INGREDIENTS

Each recipe begins with a list of the types of flowers, greenery, containers, materials, and other items you will need to complete the arrangement. For the most part, my recipes use everyday flowers that you can find almost anywhere—the grocery store, the farmers' market, even your own backyard.

TIME

Each recipe has two different time components: **Prep time** is the time it will take you to prepare the flowers and vase or container. **Cook time** is the time it will take you to arrange the flowers. The average arrangement takes about 30 minutes to make from start to finish. I've tried to include a wide variety of recipes in this book—some can be completed in a few minutes while others are more labor-intensive and will require a greater time commitment.

SEASON

The flowers you choose to include in each arrangement will depend in part on the season and availability of the blooms during that particular time of year. Specific seasons are indicated for recipes requiring flowers that are widely available only at certain times. However, many of the recipes can become year-round concoctions with some simple seasonal substitutions, or by using materials you have on hand.

LEVEL OF DIFFICULTY

Each recipe is ranked by difficulty on a scale from 1 to 4 (1 being the easiest, 4 being the most advanced). Each chapter includes recipes with varying levels of difficulty so that you can mix and match techniques that range from easy to intermediate or advanced, depending on your individual skill level and comfort with the techniques.

COST

Each recipe includes a dollar symbol representing a price range, to give you an idea of how much you will need to spend on the arrangement. The key below is only for flower cost (it doesn't include the price of the vase or container). My arrangements vary in cost, but again, they are just a starting point and you should feel free to adapt them to your own needs. Some recipes have a wider price range due to the variation in flower prices based on availability and the region where they're sold.

- $: $10 to $15
- $$: $15 to $25
- $$$: $25 to $45
- $$$$: $45 to $75

FLOWER CARE

Aspirin, sugar, a penny, bleach...what do flowers like? I get this question all the time from people wanting to know how to keep their flowers alive longer. There have been studies that test the effectiveness of all of the above, including one study that even tested flowers in soda! What I've found to be true is that flowers live the longest in plain water.

The average flower arrangement will look good for about 3 days, start to wilt at 5 days, and will need to be thrown out after a week. Tropical flowers will last much longer, 2 to 3 weeks, as will some varieties like alstroemeria, which can last up to 2 weeks.

FLOWER FOOD: TO ADD OR NOT TO ADD?

Flower food is a sugar and antibacterial mix. If your flowers come with it, go ahead and use it. I always have a small tub of it (about $5 for a small container), but I don't think it is crucial to have on hand.

Below are tips on how to best care for your flowers, along with ways to extend the life of your arrangement.

HYDRATE

Most flowers have traveled a long way to get to you, and they need to rehydrate. This is called *conditioning* in floral speak. Even if you are not going to arrange them immediately, make sure to cut the stems of the flowers and place them in cool water—not freezing cold water, which will shock them—as soon as you can.

CUT THE STEMS

Your flowers will last longer—by at least a few more days—if you cut their stems as soon as you get them home. Trim only a small amount from the bottom and cut each stem on a slant or angle—doing so creates a larger surface area, which allows the flower to drink more water. If you have a simple arrangement where you can easily take flowers out of the vase, then trim the stems every other day. Doing this and changing the water are the keys to enjoying your flowers for as long as possible.

CHANGE THE WATER

If I had to give just one piece of advice, it would be this: Change the water in the vase at least every couple days. And if not every couple days, then at least once during the lifetime of the arrangement. Flowers thrive on fresh water. To refresh the water in a small-to-medium arrangement, place the vase under the faucet in your kitchen sink and run the water so that it flushes out the old water. Flushing out your vase under the faucet refreshes the water while keeping your arrangement intact. For taller vases, carefully tilt the arrangement to pour out the old water, and refresh with new water.

REMOVE LEAVES BELOW THE WATERLINE

Always remove or "strip" leaves off any part of the stem that will be submerged in water, usually the bottom three-quarters of a stem. Besides looking sloppy, leaves that are underwater will create bacteria and kill the flowers faster.

While the bottom three-quarters of a stem should be stripped bare, it's OK to keep some leaves on the upper portion of the stem, the part above water. Whether you do so or not is simply a matter of taste—leaves can help break up a monochromatic design, which can be visually pleasing.

KEEP FLOWERS COOL

Think about the best spot to arrange flowers in terms of temperature. As long as wherever you're arranging flowers is around room temperature, your blooms will stay fresh. If it's hot, you need to put the air-conditioning on. Most flowers don't like the heat, with the exception of tropical flowers, such as orchids, which grow in warm climates. If you don't have air-conditioning and it is a hot summer day, don't work with sensitive flowers such as hydrangeas, because they will die quickly.

If you're working near a window that has direct, hot sunlight or outside on a hot day, your flowers will wilt. You can place any arrangement in the fridge for an hour or two to cool it down, but delicate flowers will get too cold and turn brown and die if you leave them in your fridge for too long. Whatever you do, though, don't put your flowers in the freezer. Any extremes in temperature, whether too cold or too hot, will kill most flowers.

REVIVE TIRED FLOWERS

If a flower seems droopy, you can sometimes revive it. Say you have a hydrangea, which is a really delicate flower. If it looks sort of sad, you can dunk the blooms in water and give it a fresh cut, and it'll perk back up that same day. But you have to catch it before the flower is actually fully wilted, because once a flower is dead, there's no bringing it back.

Also, if your roses are turning brown around the edges, you can trim the brown off the edges with scissors, following the shape of the petals. You can also trim the edges of leaves and of orchids. They'll turn brown again the next day, but I often do this, since it's worth it if you just want them to look beautiful for an event.

AVOID TOUCHING PETALS

In addition to visually checking for brownish, shriveled, or wilted petals, the best way to determine a flower's freshness is to lightly pat the top of the blossom with your palm—sort of like how you would gently squeeze peaches or plums at the grocery store to test their ripeness. A fresh bloom won't give much and will feel fairly firm to the touch. But don't overdo it—a very quick pat should be enough. The natural oil in our hands turns flowers brown and kills them (this is especially true for white flowers).

TYPES OF FLOWERS

Flowers are not all created alike. Some blooms are extremely fragrant, while others have no scent at all. Some flowers can survive a few hours out of water; others will wilt if they are without water for more than an hour.

FLOWERS THAT ARE RESILIENT OUT OF WATER

Most flowers can survive out of water for an hour, tops. The flowers listed below are more resilient, making them good for boutonnieres and floral head crowns or wreaths—anything where the stems won't be in water. They should be kept in a refrigerator overnight if they will be out of water for most of the next day (they'll last about one day out of water).

- Roses
- Spray roses
- Cymbidium orchids
- Ball dahlias
- Waxflower
- Statice
- Mums
- Carnations

HOW TO FORCE BUDS OPEN

If you'd like a pretty bouquet for your home, I'd recommend buying blooms that are slightly closed and firm so they will last longer. But if you're making an arrangement for a party, dinner, or an event, you will want the flowers to look lush and beautiful, so you should buy them as open as possible the day of or the day before your event. If your schedule permits, buy the flowers a few days ahead of your event to allow them to open naturally. Unwrap the flowers from their packaging, give the stems a fresh cut on a slant, and place in a bucket filled with about 6" to 10" of cool water.

Sometimes, though, you can't find open blooms. Maybe you can only find tightly closed buds in the flowers you want. In those cases, you can force the buds open so that on the day of the event, you have a picture-perfect arrangement. Below are two approaches to force blooms open.

1 Help the blooms open naturally. You can do this a few ways. One option is to place the stems in a bucket or vase of very warm to hot (not boiling) water to speed up the opening process. It's best to do this a day or two before you arrange the flowers, to give them a chance to open slowly. If you're arranging the flowers the same day you buy them, keep refilling the container with very warm water to force the blooms open even faster. In addition to the water trick, you can also recut the stems slightly once a day, or place the flowers near a window so that they open in natural light. Make sure, though, that they're not in full sun; otherwise the petals will wilt.

2 Physically open the blooms. If encouraging them to open naturally doesn't work, or if you buy closed blooms the day of the event, then you can try this. But be careful: The more you touch the petals, the more damaged they become, so try to work quickly with as few strokes as possible.

FOR ROUND PETALS (e.g., carnations, ranunculus, roses, anemones): Hold the flower lightly with your fingers, placing your thumb in the center of the bud. Using your thumb, push the petals outward, so that they spread out. Finally, blow on the center of the bloom to puff it out a little more.

FOR POINTY PETALS (e.g., birds of paradise, irises, oriental lilies, freesia): Pinch the tip of the bud to loosen the petals. Very gently pull each petal away from where it's attached to the bloom in a delicate peeling motion, sort of like shucking corn or peeling a banana. Some petals may break or bend if the flower is too fresh. If it's not pulling outward easily, just pinch it again and place it in warm water, then try again in a few hours. After pulling the petals, you can then blow on the middle of the flower to make it open a little more.

FLOWERS THAT ARE LONG-LASTING

The following flowers will live longer in arrangements. You should be able to get an average of 2 weeks out of them.

- Orchids
- Mums
- Mini cala lillies
- Statice
- Baby's breath
- Waxflower
- Lisianthus
- Alstroemeria

FLOWERS THAT DRY WELL

The flowers listed below look similar dried to how they look alive. Dry flowers by hanging a bouquet upside down in a cool, dark place with good ventilation. When storing, wrap the bunches in tissue paper to protect the petals from crumbling.

- Strawflowers
- Billy balls
- Statice
- Baby's breath
- Coxcomb
- Thistle
- Lotus pods
- Clover

FLOWERS THAT ARE EXPENSIVE

If you want to use expensive flowers but are on a budget, use fewer of the pricier blooms as a focal point in an arrangement or bouquet. Some more expensive flowers include:

- Garden roses
- Peonies
- Lily of the valley
- Amaryllis
- Casablanca lilies
- Hellebores

FLOWERS THAT ARE FRAGRANT

The flowers listed below all smell wonderful. Sometimes, though, you don't want your arrangements to have any scent, such as for a seated dinner party or when bringing a bouquet to a friend in the hospital. In those cases, you'll probably want to avoid using these flowers:

- Gardenias
- Narcissus
- Sweet peas
- Lily of the valley
- Hyacinths
- Lilacs
- Lavender
- Jasmine vines
- Verbena vines
- Tuberose
- Roses
- Lilies
- Freesia
- Chocolate cosmos

SUBSTITUTIONS

Whenever I do an event or a wedding, I make sure to tell the client that no matter how far in advance I order the flowers, they may become unavailable at the last minute due to unpredictable circumstances, such as weather. In these cases, I find other flowers that can achieve a similar overall look. The following are reasonable swaps based on comparable color, shape, and price. Substitute:

- Garden roses for peonies
- Chrysanthemums for dahlias
- Ranunculus for roses
- Stock for hydrangeas
- Tulips for mini calla lilies

FLOWERS BY SEASON AND COLOR

The charts below are general guides to common cut flowers by season and by color. Keep in mind that where you live will determine when you can get certain flowers. Most out-of-season flowers can be special-ordered and imported from around the world, but be prepared to pay at least 3 times the normal cost.

FLOWERS BY SEASON

FLOWER	FALL	WINTER	SPRING	SUMMER
ALSTROEMERIA	X	X	X	X
AMARANTHUS	X	X	X	X
AMARYLLIS		X	X	
ANEMONE		X	X	
ANTHURIUM	X	X	X	X
CALLA LILY	X	X	X	X
CARNATION	X	X	X	X
DAHLIA	X		X	X
DELPHINIUM			X	X
FREESIA	X	X	X	X
GERBERA DAISY	X	X	X	X
GLADIOLUS	X	X	X	X
HYACINTH		X	X	
HYDRANGEA	X	X	X	X
IRIS	X	X	X	X
LISIANTHUS	X	X	X	X
MUM	X	X	X	X
ORCHID	X	X	X	X
RANUNCULUS	X	X	X	
ROSE	X	X	X	X
STATICE	X	X	X	X
SWEET PEA		X	X	
TULIP	X	X	X	X

FLOWERS BY COLOR

FLOWER	RED	ORANGE	YELLOW	PINK	PEACH	GREEN	BLUE	PURPLE	WHITE
ALSTROEMERIA	X	X	X	X	X	X		X	X
AMARANTHUS	X					X			
AMARYLLIS	X	X		X	X				X
ANEMONE	X			X			X	X	X
ANTHURIUM	X	X		X	X	X		X	X
CALLA LILY (MINI)	X	X	X	X	X			X	X
CARNATION	X	X	X	X	X	X		X	X
DAHLIA	X	X	X	X	X			X	X
DELPHINIUM							X	X	X
FREESIA	X	X	X	X	X			X	X
GERBERA DAISY	X	X	X	X	X				X
GLADIOLUS	X	X	X	X	X	X		X	X
HYACINTH				X	X			X	X
HYDRANGEA	X			X		X	X	X	X
IRIS			X				X	X	X
LISIANTHUS			X	X				X	X
MUM	X	X	X			X			X
ORCHID	X	X	X	X	X	X		X	X
RANUNCULUS	X	X	X	X	X	X		X	X
ROSE	X	X	X	X	X	X		X	X
STATICE			X	X	X			X	X
SWEET PEA	X			X	X			X	X
TULIP	X	X	X	X	X	X		X	X

GREENS

Greenery is used to fill out a vase, to add color and texture, and to complement the flowers in an arrangement. Below are the most common greens used in floral design.

Lemon leaves: This is the most frequently used greenery. You can get a large bunch at very little cost ($3 to $5).

Hypericum ("coffee-bean" berry): Hypericum are stems that have tiny berries attached (reminiscent of coffee beans, hence the nickname). They are very common and usually come in brown, green, and white varieties. They can, in fact, smell like coffee!

Bupleurum: These leaves are wispy and delicate. They have a naturally wild look to them—almost vine-like. You should be careful when using them because while they're fairly long-lasting, they will wilt quickly if they're near heat or direct sunlight.

Ti leaves: Often used to line vases, these leaves are long and wide, and very long-lasting. They're usually available in shades of green, but they also come in reds and a gorgeous black.

Eucalyptus: This helps an arrangement look a little more rustic. Its color is a silvery green, and it smells wonderful. Since the leaves are sticky, when stripping the bottom leaves for an arrangement it's often easier to use a floral knife or kitchen knife than your hands. Varieties include seeded, silver dollar, and regular.

Bear grass: Long and pliable, this greenery is inexpensive and long-lasting. Steel grass is the stiff, thicker version, but it's expensive and hard to find.

Monstera leaves: These are the big tropical leaves that look like fans. Although they're not always readily available, they are commonly used in larger arrangements. They're usually sold individually.

Horsetail: This is a very thin form of bamboo. In some regions it grows wild. Use it in Asian-inspired arrangements or to line a vase.

Ruscus: This comes in two types, Israeli and Italian (which looks a little smaller and more delicate). Both are thin stems with leaves going down the entire length, making them a great choice to elongate an arrangement or add texture. They are a true green color.

Fern: This is another wispy type of greenery most often used as a filler base.

Solidaster: Wispy and reminiscent of ferns, these lime-green leaves provide a quick way to brighten up an arrangement. They also come in a light brown color. They are easy to find and long-lasting. Remove any excess greenery from the bottom half of the stem before using.

Dusty miller: This greenery is usually sold in shorter bunches. It is very useful for softening an arrangement. Another similar-looking type of greenery is called lamb's ear because of its curvy, gray, super-soft petals.

MOSS

There are many types of moss; I've listed the most common types below. Moss is sold dried or fresh, although fresh is harder to find. It can be used to cover exposed floral foam or for decorative purposes.

Sheet moss: This is the most common type of moss (you'll find it in any craft store, floral supply store, or florist), and it does actually come in sheet form. It is very flat and thin, and useful for covering mistakes or wrapping around a basket handle.

Mood moss: This moss is available in large chunks, and it's very thick and fluffy. It is also expensive. I prefer to buy it fresh from a wholesaler, but if you soak the dried kind, it looks just as good.

Spanish moss: This moss comes in gray and green (when dried) and light green (when fresh). It is stringy, resembling ramen noodles.

Reindeer moss: This moss is spongy and is usually sold in smaller packages than other mosses are. It is most commonly found in a lime-green color, although dyed reindeer moss can be red and burnt orange, and sometimes it's also available in navy and dark green.

CURLY WILLOW

These branches have so many uses. They can be curled inside vases for more natural arrangements, they can be used to help keep flowers in place, they can be shaped into handles for baskets, or they can simply be placed in a large vase, urn, or other container by themselves for a more organic look. They come in bunches of 5 to 10 stems, in heights ranging from 3 feet to 8 feet tall. Buy them fresh, so that they are more pliant. Trim the ends before using.

BUYING BASICS

Before you rush out to buy an armful of flowers, first take into account where you might go to get those blooms and what else you might need to arrange them. From grocery stores to florists, there are a number of places where you can buy flowers, and I've outlined the differences below—along with some supplies that might be helpful to have on hand.

HOW MUCH TO BUY

You don't want to overbuy, because you don't want to waste flowers—and money—but you don't want to underbuy, because that can leave you stuck in a jam. I find that a good rule of thumb for buying is to use the following basic trick: Cup your hands above the top of the vase, as wide as the desired circumference of the arrangement. When you buy flowers, cup your hands above the bunches to see how many stems you'll need to buy.

Keep in mind that you'll inevitably lose one or two blooms; I can't tell you how many times I'll be making an arrangement and a flower snaps. If I really need that particular flower, then I will wire the stem. It won't last, because it can't get water, but if there's a hole in an arrangement and you really need it, it'll at least get you through.

If you're buying flowers for your home or to give as a bouquet, and you want them to be more tightly closed so that they last longer, keep in mind that you'll need to buy more blooms—tighter buds take up less space than fully open blossoms.

WHOLESALERS

Wholesalers distribute flowers. They can be the middleman between the grower and consumer (retail florists or the general public), or the growers can be their own distributors. Flower marts and farmers' markets both host wholesalers. These are good places to get deals on large amounts of flowers if you're doing arrangements for a wedding or another big event.

Flowers are almost always sold in bunches at flower marts and farmers' markets, though some expensive and exotic flowers such as amaryllis, cymbidium orchids, and anthurium are sold by the stem. Wholesale roses are sold in bunches by stem length, starting at 40 centimeters for shorter stems, then going to 50, 60, and finally 70 for superlong stems.

Bigger cities usually have flower marts. Check online to find out if there's a flower mart near you, and if there is, see if they allow the public to buy there. Some flower marts have special days or hours for the general public, and some marts allow only floral industry people in. I recommend going as early as possible to get the best flowers—if I'm not there by 8 a.m., I consider myself late. Walk around and see which vendors have flowers you like. Since there are so many similar flowers all in one space (especially in flower marts), prices are pretty comparable. It's really just a matter of which seller draws you in and whose flowers you prefer.

I have a few insider tips for when you're shopping the flower mart. First, keep in mind that flowers with very open blooms are going to be cheaper, since they have shorter life spans. They'll only last a day or two, because they're so open, but if you have a Friday or Saturday event, you can often get a discount for the lushest, most open blooms, since the vendor wants to get rid of them before the new week's shipment arrives. For example, with garden roses (which are gorgeous, smell amazing, and are usually really expensive), you can often get them on the weekend for a third of the weekday price. Also, sometimes, vendors keep the freshest flowers tucked away in their coolers. I always ask. And finally, if you have a particular flower in mind and don't see it displayed, wholesalers can special-order blooms for you, which should be done at least a week in advance of your event.

Even if there's no flower mart near you or it's not open to the public, there will probably be a farmers' market or a pick-your-own farm in your area that will happily sell quality flowers directly to you at prices much cheaper than most florists can offer.

RETAILERS

When you're not buying direct from the farmer or from a wholesaler, then you're generally buying retail. Flowers are sold at a retail level through florists, as well as through grocery stores, home improvement stores, and some general big-box stores. As with anything retail, remember that there's a wide range of what's out there. Some high-end grocery stores or small artisanal food markets might have better-quality flowers than really low-end florists. It just depends. But based on overall generalizations, I've outlined the major differences between the two kinds of retailers.

Florists

Florists sell flowers by the stem. Generally, the price will be about 2.5 to 3 times more expensive than at a wholesaler. So if they buy a bunch of hydrangea (5 stems) for $7.50 ($1.50/stem), the florist will sell it to the walk-in customer for $4.50/stem. For arrangements, each florist has their own markup depending on the quality, region, and style they specialize in, ranging anywhere from 2.5 to 4 times the wholesale cost.

With florists, you're paying for convenience. If you're short on time and need a quick arrangement made, or you don't live near a craft store, then you can pop into a florist and pick up a ready-made bouquet or buy a block of floral foam. But you'll pay more for that convenience.

Florists are also good places to order exotic flowers or to find out-of-season flowers. And finally, higher-end florists do take good care of their flowers. They give the flowers fresh cuts, condition them, and regularly change their water.

Grocery, Home Improvement, and Big-Box Stores

These stores sell their flowers mostly by the bunch, although the occasional place does also sell by the stem. For most of us, picking up household items on the way home from the office or stopping by the grocery to get food, it's super-simple to just toss a few bunches of flowers in our cart while we're doing our other shopping. I buy grocery flowers all the time. Though the quality can be mixed and variety can be limited, you can find good flowers here—usually at lower prices than florists, and sometimes even as cheap as at wholesalers.

ORGANIC, LOCAL, AMERICAN-GROWN, AND FAIR TRADE

It is always best to buy local. It means that you're not only supporting farmers in your area, but you're also getting the freshest flowers possible. Many flowers that are out of season locally or in the States can still be bought from a wholesaler, but the prices soar dramatically and the quality usually isn't as good. If you're doing a big event, you can place an advance order with a local supplier at a farmers' market. You will, however, be limited to what they're growing at that particular time, which is why florists mainly buy from large wholesalers. I also encourage you to buy American-grown flowers. Some labels to look for are American Grown, California's CA Grown, or your own state's label for locally grown flowers.

Flowers can be certified as sustainably grown, fair trade, and organic in much the same way as food. These designations mean the flowers were grown with consideration for workers and the environment, along with reduced use of pesticides (or none in the case of organic certification). Some labels to look for on the plastic packaging include Fair Trade, Veriflora, and Rainforest Alliance. As of now, roses, carnations, and daisies are the most prevalent Fair Trade–certified flowers, and they usually come from Central or South America.

SUPPLIES

I'm assuming that you are arranging flowers at home—on your kitchen counter as I often do or on your dining room table—and not in a fancy studio. I certainly don't expect that you'll have a toolbox or workspace specifically for flowers, nor do you even need one for the recipes in this book. Below are the elements every flower chef needs in the pantry. Some you'll need to go out and buy (craft stores, floral supply stores, and online sites sell what's listed below), but I bet you'll be surprised at what you can do with items you already own. It's not unusual for me to just grab a pair of household scissors and a steak knife when I'm arranging flowers at home.

VASES

Nearly anything can be used as a vase. There are a variety of vases in this book, but as you look through the recipes you'll see that I reuse a lot of them. I mainly use low square or round vases, medium or tall cylinder or rectangle vases, medium-sized ceramic square vases, metallic vases, and wooden boxes. You can always substitute whichever vase you have. In a pinch, I've spray-painted clear vases gold for holiday events, and I often grab a juice glass when I don't have a cylinder vase handy.

In other words, be creative! A cowboy boot, a large shoe box, or a French press could be made into a vase. Start looking at everyday household items for inspiration. In your kitchen, use serving bowls, pitchers, a child's colorful bowl, and teapots as vases. Even if it doesn't hold water, don't rule anything out. You can always put a plastic liner, a small vase, or a little soup bowl filled with floral foam inside. How about that fedora in the closet, or the basket that usually holds magazines? You'll be surprised by all your options.

FLORAL FOAM

I call floral foam training wheels for flowers because once you insert a stem a few inches into the foam it stays put, making arranging much easier. Floral foam is sold dry in brick form. Once it is soaked and the foam completely absorbs the water, the foam gets heavier, which is good for stability inside vases. And the flowers drink the water from the foam. Be sure to buy the foam intended for fresh flowers, not artificial flowers.

SCISSORS

You can use any kind of scissors to cut flowers. But proper floral clippers [a], which look like a cross between garden pruners and regular scissors, are helpful. Household scissors are usually flimsier than floral clippers, and floral clippers cut through thicker stems and branches more easily. You can pick up an affordable pair of proper floral clippers at a craft store or a floral supply store, and discount dollar stores also sometimes carry them.

PRUNERS

For thick stems like hydrangeas or for branches, garden pruners [b] come in handy. You can also use these instead of floral clippers, but they are bigger and I find them more unwieldy than compact floral clippers when trimming thinner-stemmed flowers like tulips and sweet peas. You might already use a pair of these for gardening, and they're easy to find at home improvement stores and nurseries, as well as floral supply stores.

KNIVES

Most florists have knives in their toolbox. You can buy a straight floral knife [c], or simply use a Swiss army knife [d]. Knives can be used to run down the length of a stem to remove thorns and leaves. Florists also often use knives to cut flower stems, because you can get really fast at it with lots of practice, but I'm clumsy and prefer to use clippers or scissors. I've never noticed a difference in the longevity of the flowers whether I trim the bottom of the stems with a knife or with scissors.

ROSE STRIPPER [e]

If you are working with a ton of roses or really dislike thorns, this is a handy tool. It's a small metal or plastic gizmo with two prongs that you close around the top of the rose stem near the bloom, then quickly pull down the length of the stem, removing the thorns as you go. You can usually get these for under $5 at floral supply stores or online.

TAPE

I highly recommend buying floral tape (several kinds, listed below) and keeping it on hand. I'm all for using household items to replace specialized tools, but there are truly no substitutions for the real thing in this case. Don't even try using household transparent tape—it won't work.

Clear floral tape [f] will help you immensely and I encourage you to buy a couple rolls. It comes in a variety of thicknesses (I like to use a narrow ¼" one). I mainly use it to create grids on the top of vases, which keep stems in place. Also, I sometimes use it to secure a bouquet if I'm dropping it into a clear vase.

Floral stem tape [g] is a green tape that's self-sticking, thin, and lightweight, and I use it for boutonnieres, floral crowns, and wiring stems.

Thick green floral tape [h] (also called bowl tape) is what I use to secure bouquets. Other florists tend to use the floral stem tape because it creates a smooth surface, but I like to use this kind because it is heavier, sturdier, and waterproof. I also use this to secure floral foam to a plastic dish.

WIRE AND TWINE

You will need different types of wire and twine at times to accomplish various flower-arrangement tasks, some of which are mentioned below. Clear elastic ponytail holders and rubber bands are also very useful for holding arrangements together.

Straight stem wire [i], also called straight green floral wire, comes in different gauges, most commonly ranging from 16 gauge (thicker) to 30 gauge (thinner). I like to have straight wire in a 20 to 22 gauge range for wiring flowers, floral crowns, and to create pins to secure moss into foam. You buy this in precut packs, with each piece of wire measuring 18" long.

Metallic spooled wire [k]: A spool of thin silver or gold wire is helpful to have around. You can use it to attach moss to baskets as well as for decorative purposes. I use thinner gauges of this, such as 24-gauge wire.

Decorative aluminum wire [l]: This is a thick aluminum wire that comes in different gauges, most commonly ranging from 6 gauge (thickest) to 12 gauge (slightly thinner). It is sturdy and malleable, making it useful to secure bouquets and to add inside a vase for decorative purposes.

Twine [m]: I prefer twine that has a thin wire in it. The wire gives it shape and makes it easier to use. You can use twine to tie bouquets or to attach flowers to a post or chair.

WATER TUBES [n]

Sometimes, certain blooms in an arrangement don't have stems long enough to reach water or foam. In those cases, plastic water tubes can be attached to each stem. Often sold in packages of a hundred, one bag of these should last you a while. I generally buy tubes with pointy ends, to make them easier to slide

Bullion wire [j]: This is a really thin wire that comes as a spool of 28-gauge silver or gold and is used for decorative purposes, such as to bunch up inside a vase.

between other flowers or to stick into floral foam. If the flower stem is too thick to fit into the water tube, cut two slits across from each other in the opening of the water tube to enlarge the opening (see photo on page 143).

FLORAL PICKS (ALSO CALLED HYACINTH STICKS) [o]

If a flower has a really short stem—or you just want the stem to be even longer—you would place the stem in the water tube, then use the thick green floral tape to attach the water tube to a floral pick. These green, wooden picks give your flower that much more length. Picks are also helpful when you're using fruit or other produce. Just poke the pick into your lemon, lime, or whatever item you're using, then stick it into your arrangement.

CORSAGE PINS [p]

It's a good idea to have a box of corsage pins on hand to secure ribbon. They come in a variety of colors. Traditional corsage pins have a slightly larger pearl head and are about 2″ long, whereas boutonniere pins are 1.5″ long and have a smaller round head. They often come in white, black, and silver. If the pin is too long and will stick all the way through the bouquet, you can cut it shorter using floral scissors or wire cutters.

RIBBON [q]

Nicer ribbon does make a difference. I recommend thick satin ribbon, which holds up well and looks pretty. Since you can buy a yard or two of it at some craft stores, instead of a whole spool, it's easy to run out and get ribbon in whatever color you want when you have a certain arrangement in mind. I also like using wired ribbon, since it keeps its shape if I'm making a bow.

LEAF SHINE

This comes in a spray can, and there are many different brands. Leaves are often dusty, and even with a paper towel, you can't really clean them. So if you want an arrangement to look very professional and shiny, you use this just like you would use hair spray, spraying it on leaves from about 10″ away. But don't put this on fresh flowers—it is only meant for greenery. Use only on arrangements where foliage and greenery are a prominent part, such as a tropical arrangement where you're showcasing the leaves.

FLORAL PRESERVATIVE SPRAY

If I could choose only one option between leaf shine and floral preservative spray, I'd choose the latter. This is fine to use on flowers or greenery, and it gives flowers a nice gleam, which is perfect for larger events.

ADHESIVES

Some arrangements use general household adhesives, such as clear glue or hot glue. But there's one specialty adhesive, clay tape, that is waterproof, making it the perfect adhesive to secure LED votives to the bottom of the vase or to attach a plastic foam-filled dish to a tall vase for a statement piece.

2

FLOWER PREP AND DESIGN FUNDAMENTALS

Now you know the basic tools you'll need to get started. The next step is getting the flowers ready to arrange. In this chapter, I'll show you how to prep many types of flowers, as well as give you overall design pointers and ideas to consider before you dive into the actual arranging.

One tip to remember no matter what flower you use or what design technique you're trying: Don't forget to put water in the vase. It sounds silly to mention, but I'm always surprised how many people forget this basic first step when they're putting together an arrangement. I usually fill a vase about three-quarters full of water, because when you add flowers, it'll raise the waterline. If you're going to transport an arrangement, fill your vase only halfway, then add the rest of the water when you arrive at your destination. Make filling your vase with water your automatic first step of any arrangement, unless I specify otherwise in a recipe.

FLOWER PREPARATION

Flower prep is one of the most important things you can do (besides changing the water daily) to help your arrangements last longer and look their best. Readying flowers and vases for arrangements is the most time-consuming part of floral design. The arranging, especially with practice, goes fairly quickly.

Below are prep instructions for most of the flowers used in the book. Note that these are cut flowers, and might vary in color or size. These instructions will eventually become second nature to you, as you practice more and more, but until then, refer back to this section whenever you have questions on how to prep specific flowers.

Unless otherwise indicated, prep all flowers as one of the very first things you do for each recipe. Think of it like chopping, mincing, and measuring ingredients before you begin cooking.

ALSTROEMERIAS

Sometimes referred to as Peruvian lilies, this is a very easy-to-find flower that is mostly used as filler in an arrangement. But as with any cheaper flower, to make them look more expensive, buy a huge bunch of them. Alstroemerias look stunning if you use them alone, pulling together a ton of just one color in a beautiful vase. To prep them, strip off the leaves by quickly running your hand down the stem (against the natural growth of the leaves). They'll fall off easily.

AMARANTHUS

Amaranthus comes in sage green, plum/red, and brown. They're naturally draping and often called hanging amaranthus. Some have lots of foliage. Remove any leaves that would be below the waterline.

ANEMONES

Anemones are round flowers that look similar to poppies. They open wide into a nearly perfect circle that usually has a darker center. They're delicate and sensitive to heat. Easy to prep since they have no greenery, just give them a small cut at the end of the stems.

ANTHURIUMS

These are tropical flowers that have one bloom on each stem. They are shiny and look almost rubbery. They come in a variety of colors, most often in pink, red, green, and white. There's no greenery on these, so to prep, they just need a small cut at the end of their stems.

BELLS OF IRELAND

This long green flower has groups of small blooms with thorns inside along the length of the stem. Strip off the bottom blooms using a downward motion, but be careful as you may get slightly pricked (see photo on page 28). Note that the top, pointy part of the flower is sensitive to heat and wilts easily.

BILLY BALLS

Billy balls (craspedia) are yellow balls on a thin stem with no greenery. These are great for adding texture or visual interest to an arrangement. The ends of the stems can be given a fresh cut.

CALLA LILIES

Calla lilies are very elegant flowers that are tall, lean, and have one fluted bloom. There is no foliage on the stems; you only have to give the stems a quick cut before putting them in water. They are fairly long-lasting, and the mini variety is good to use in hot weather.

Regular (large): Calla lilies are usually white, though there is a kelly-green variety that is a bit harder to find.

Mini: These are also called New Zealand calla lilies. They come in nearly every color, ranging from light pastels to deep jewel tones. They are hardy and keep up well in the heat.

CAMPANULAS

Campanula has bell-shaped blossoms with soft greenery and comes in a variety of pastel colors: yellow, pink, purple, and white. This flower is very sensitive to heat. To prep, remove any greenery that will be below the waterline by stripping off the leaves with your hand in a downward motion.

CARNATIONS

Carnations are very hardy and last a long time both in and out of water. They come in a mini (1") and regular (2" to 3") size, and in all colors of the rainbow. Remove any greenery by pulling downward or using a knife to scrape off the leaves. Open carnation blooms by placing your thumb in the center and gently pushing the petals outward.

CHRYSANTHEMUMS

Super-hardy, these flowers are sold in large bunches and are generally inexpensive. You prep them by stripping off the bottom two-thirds of any leaves on the stem with your hand. There are many different types of mums, a few of which are explained below.

Button mums / Pompoms: These are small blooms and they are very hardy. They are often used for ring-bearer pillows, pomander balls, and in wildflower arrangements.

China mums: These have round, fluffy petals. They are very sensitive to heat and will wilt fast.

Spider mums: These have very slender, pointy petals.

DAHLIAS

Delightful flowers that go with everything, these blooms are round with many small petals that splay outward from their centers. A regular dahlia is about 2" to 3" wide, and sensitive to heat. Dahlias usually have a lot of foliage on them, and 2 to 3 smaller stems with flowers on each main stem. (If there are extra little buds that are

tightly closed on dahlias, they won't open, no matter how much you try and force them.) Remove excess leaves from the bottom half of the stem, then cut off any secondary stems from the main stem, setting the trimmed blooms aside for later use or to put in bud vases.

Dinner plate: These light and fluffy flowers are very large, spanning 5" to 6". They are very sensitive to heat and will wilt fast in direct sunlight.

Ball: These are about the same size as regular dahlias, except the petals are very stiff and are tightly clustered. They are a very hardy flower and will last in the heat and also out of water, making them perfect for summer events, boutonnieres, and bouquets.

DELPHINIUMS

Delphiniums come in blue, white, and purple. They are tall, thin stems covered in many blooms. They can be sensitive to heat. Remove any blooms or foliage that will be below the waterline by stripping them off with your hand using a downward motion.

FREESIAS

Freesia is a delicate thin-stemmed flower, popular for its sweet fragrance. It requires little prep, just a small cut on the end of its stems.

GERBERA DAISIES

The vividly colored blooms of these daisies are 3" to 4" wide and have many petals going around the center. They can be sensitive to heat. When they're older, the petals will start to fall off. They have no leaves, so to prep, just give them a small cut at the ends of the stems.

GLADIOLI

Gladioli have long stems with blooms going down the entire stem. To encourage blooms to open, pinch off and remove the very top closed bloom. Remove any blooms or greenery that will be below the waterline by cutting or pulling them off from the main stem.

the flower chef

HYACINTHS

With these short flowers that come with bulbs attached, it's best to leave the bulb on, although sometimes it's necessary to remove everything from the stem to fit the flower in a vase. Hyacinths have many tiny blooms along the main stem, and fresh hyacinths have tight blooms that will become very fragrant when open. To prep, just give them a fresh cut at the end of the stem if you do detach the bulb.

HYDRANGEAS

The flowers I get asked about most are hydrangeas because they wilt very quickly, especially in the heat. At room temperature they are fine, but they can't be in a hot room or in the sun.

Never buy soft hydrangeas (if they're soft, they're not fresh). Place your open hand lightly on top of the flower head; it should be firm to the touch.

Hydrangeas have thick, woody stems, which can be hard to cut on a slant. Some florists use a hammer and pound the bottom inch until it splinters, but I prefer to take scissors and cut a few vertical slices up into the bottom of the stem. I can't say this enough: Hydrangeas love water!

The real trick is that in addition to cutting or pounding the stems, you need to run the flower heads under the faucet so that they're well soaked or dunk the blooms in a bucket of water and gently shake off the excess water. Hydrangeas drink through their petals, and running water over them when prepping them will make a huge difference to how long they last. After they've all been arranged in the vase, use a spray bottle to frequently spray them with water (or spray them with a floral preservative).

Remove the leaves by snapping them off with your thumb, pushing them down against the stem. Take off any leaves that are below the waterline or any that will make it difficult to poke the stem through a taped grid. Depending on the look you want, you can leave on a few leaves just below the bloom to add a pop of green to an arrangement, but make sure to remove any leaves that have holes or browning around the edges.

Regular hydrangeas: Hydrangeas come in white and a variety of colors, from pastels (sage, pink, blue) to dark (antique reds and greens). They are light and fluffy, and have a large head, which makes them very economical as they are inexpensive and take up a lot of surface space.

Mini green hydrangeas: These are lime green and are the baby form of the white hydrangeas. The blooms are stiff and very short. Unlike regular hydrangeas, these are very hardy and good to use in hot weather. You don't need to soak the heads of these hydrangeas in water.

IRISES

Irises are pointy flowers that usually come in white, blue, or purple. The blooms are tightly closed when fresh. To force iris blooms open, lightly pinch the tips of the blooms and pull the outer petals gently downward, as if you're peeling a banana—this will encourage the petals to open fully. Remove excess leaves by pulling them down off the stem. Give them a fresh cut on the ends of their stems.

LILIES

This classic flower is one of the most fragrant, and comes in numerous varieties. The most important thing to remember when prepping them is to remove the pollen from the stamens as soon as the buds open; otherwise the pollen will fall off and stain whatever it touches. Quickly pinch off the pollen with your fingers, or use a tissue or paper towel if you don't want your fingers stained bright yellow, brown, or orange for a few days. If you do get some pollen on your clothes, you can often immediately pat it off with household tape or packing tape.

Lilies have soft, green leaves that can be removed by swiping your fingers down the stems like you would with rosemary, or using your thumb to snap them off downward. Then use a knife to gently scrape along the stem to remove any last bits of leaves and to make sure the stem is perfectly clean and smooth.

Oriental and Asiatic lilies: These are the most popular types of lilies, coming in a wide variety of colors ranging from whites and yellows to eye-popping pinks and oranges. Oriental lilies usually have a strong fragrance; Asiatic lilies generally have no smell.

Casablanca lilies: These are white lilies that open widely and are very expensive. You can recognize them by the small, white, raised spots that cover each petal.

LISIANTHUSES

These flowers have thin stems, with multiple stems attached to a main one. They have fluffy open blooms that often look droopy and like they are about to wilt, but that's just their nature. Lisianthus generally have a lot of foliage. Remove the leaves by stripping them off using a downward motion, like you do with lilies. For modern designs that have precise lines, cut off the lower blooms attached to the main stem on the lisianthus so that a single stem has only a single bloom, setting the trimmed blooms aside for later use or to put in bud vases. For a wildflower arrangement or rustic designs, remove the shorter stems and blooms from the main stem so that the remaining blooms are close in height to each other.

They are inexpensive and very long-lasting, although by the time you take off all the greenery and extra stems, you're not left with a lot, so keep that in mind when you're buying. They are a good fit for a wildflower arrangement or rustic designs.

PEONIES

Usually available in whites, pinks, and burgundies, peonies have a short season at the end of spring and beginning of summer. The blooms are tightly closed when fresh and can open completely within a day, depending on temperature. They have very light, if any, foliage. Remove any excess leaves or brown petals from the outer part of the flower.

PROTEAS

Proteas are tropical flowers with spiky petals. They are very hardy and long-lasting. There are many varieties of protea, but the most common is called pincushion, which looks like its name and comes in red, orange, and yellow. Another variety is king protea, which is a lot larger and commonly white with a pink edge. They all have tough green leaves going down the stem. To prep, remove any greenery that will be below the waterline by stripping off the leaves in a downward motion with your hand, or just pull them off. Gently scrape any excess leaves off the stem using a knife.

RANUNCULUSES

These round flowers are small and have circular layered petals. They don't need much prep. Simply remove any loose leaves, or any leaves from the bottom half of the stem. Ranunculus come in many different sizes and colors and are fairly long-lasting. If you are looking for an alternative to a rose, this is a good choice.

ROSES

Check each rose for bruised outer petals, plucking off any bruised petals from the blossoms and discarding. Fresh roses are firm when lightly patted. Remove the leaves and thorns from the stem by sliding a small paring knife, Swiss army knife, or rose stripper down the stem, using some force. If the roses don't have thorns, you can remove the leaves by stripping them off with your hands in a downward motion. I like to remove all but a few leaves at the top. Try not to get a lot of water on the rose heads—they don't like that.

There are thousands of varieties of roses; some buds never open, while others open fast and live a long time. Most don't have a strong fragrance because they're mass-produced.

Garden roses: These are very fragrant and very expensive specialty roses that open wide with a swirl of petals at the center.

Spray roses: These are the very small roses, about half or a third the size of regular roses, with multiple blooms on tiny stems attached to the main stem. Garden roses also come in spray form, although those aren't as easy to find.

'SAFARI SUNSET'/'SAFARI GOLDSTRIKE'

These are tropical-looking, pointy flowers with blooms going down the entire stem. 'Safari Sunset' is usually red or brown and 'Safari Goldstrike' is usually white or green. Remove any blooms that will be below the waterline by using your hands to push them off in a downward motion.

SNAPDRAGONS

Snapdragons have long stems with numerous small flowers on the top half. They have light foliage on the entire stem. Strip off the leaves [a] by quickly running your hand down the stem (against the natural growth of the leaves), just like you would strip stalks of rosemary. Then use a knife to gently scrape along the stem to remove any last bits of leaves and to make sure the stem is perfectly clean and smooth. [b]

STAR OF BETHLEHEM

Star of Bethlehem flowers look like asparagus when their buds are tightly closed. When they bloom, the white flowers open and resemble tuberose or jasmine. Give them a small cut at the end.

STATICE

Statice already looks dried and can feel brittle. There are many tiny blooms on each stem, and many smaller stems clustered together at the top of each main one. The stems often have bits of excess greenery. To prep them, use a knife to scrape along the stem to make sure it's clean.

STOCK

Stock is a great flower to practice with, because it's inexpensive and an easy-to-find filler flower. It has soft, light green foliage and many blooms ranging from light whites and pastels to deep plum and purples, and like hydrangeas, this flower takes up a lot of space in an arrangement. Remove the leaves as you would with lilies and snapdragons by placing your thumb with your index and middle fingers at the top of the foliage (a few inches below the flower) and swiftly pulling downward, removing the leaves in one quick motion.

SUNFLOWERS

Sunflowers have large blooms and require minimal prep. Simply remove any brown leaves or extra foliage below the bloom.

THISTLES

The most commonly found variety of thistle is blue. These are a spiky flower, with many blooms attached to the main stem. Remove any excess greenery on the lower half of the stem by pulling it off.

TUBEROSES

Tuberoses are highly fragrant with tiny white flowers that look similar to jasmine. The flowers run along the top half of each tuberose stem. When they're wilted, the blooms shrivel and turn brown. If using that day, pick out ones that are already bloomed; otherwise, I recommend buying stems with closed blooms.

TULIPS

If tulips are open, you can put them in the fridge to close them back up a little. Heat expands tulips and opens them up. A fun fact: This is a flower that grows after it's cut. If you make a beautiful arrangement that's all the same height, and you come back the next day, the tulips will be poking their heads up higher than the rest of the flowers. You can just give the stems a quick trim so they're level again with the other flowers.

To prep tulips, peel off the leaves by stripping them off with your hand—like you're peeling a banana. Tulips usually have dirt at the bottom of their stems and in between their leaves, so after you've removed the leaves, either run the stems under the faucet or rub off the dirt with a damp paper towel. Then use a knife to gently scrape along the stem to remove any last bits of leaves and to make sure the stem is perfectly clean and smooth.

Dutch tulips: These are the basic, short tulips you see most often.

French tulips: These are long-stemmed tulips with a larger head and very smooth, buttery-looking petals. They come in pastel colors and are usually double the price of Dutch tulips.

Parrot tulips: These tulips are short like Dutch ones, except they have a fringed, scalloped edge. They are often two-toned and are a bit more expensive than Dutch.

VIBURNUMS

Viburnums resemble hydrangeas, with small clusters of tiny blooms that droop slightly from the main stem. They're seasonal to spring, and they cost about 2 to 3 times the price of hydrangeas. There's light foliage. If there are leaves, remove any that would sit below the waterline.

WAXFLOWERS

Waxflowers have many tiny stems covered in small buds. Though they look delicate, they're actually quite hardy. The leaves look like rosemary and can be difficult to take off. Use a bit of force to remove them by either pulling them off or by taking a knife and scraping them off the main stem.

DESIGN TECHNIQUES

There are countless ways to arrange flowers. The design techniques I use most frequently are spiraling, utilizing floral foam, making a taped grid, and lining a vase. When you get more advanced, you can make floral designs without the help of aids such as floral foam and taped grids (as you'll learn in the Freehand Arrangements chapter), but that takes a lot of practice (and patience).

Beyond the tried-and-true techniques, I also developed some of my own for efficiency because, like you, I'm busy, and I wanted to make arrangements that anyone could replicate. The following information will come in handy as you start to design.

BASIC COLOR COMBINATION RULES

For many people, mixing and matching colors can be tricky. But I think that part of the fun of floral design is choosing which colors to use. A lot of color mixing is just holding up different combinations next to each other to see what you like; after all, so much of flower arranging is about your own taste. I personally love the way yellow and green look together. Play around with colors, and after a while, you'll find your own favorite mixed hues. But if you'd like some guidance, here are some simple rules of thumb that make color combinations easy:

Monochromatic: Use a variety of flowers in one color, or use one type of flower in varying shades of the same color.

Complementary colors: Remember the color wheel from art class? Use it as a guide and you can't go wrong, combining colors that appear across from each other on the wheel: orange and blue, purple and yellow, green and red. You can also add an optional contrasting color (something vibrant or jewel toned) for an accent.

Highlights: For an unexpected combination, use a hint of color in one flower to inspire another choice of blooms. For example, if you're using white alstroemerias with a slightly yellow center, look for a yellow flower such as yellow roses, calla lilies, or sunflowers for a lovely pairing. After all, if the combination looks good in nature, it'll look great in your arrangement.

Dark tones: For a darker, wintery, or bolder look, use deeper jewel tones as contrasting colors in your arrangement. In fact, I like adding darker, almost black colors to give arrangements some depth. For example, a white, green, and plum bouquet is a gorgeous combination. Keep in mind that any flowers that are called "black" (e.g., black dahlias, black mini calla lilies, 'Black Baccara' roses) aren't really a true black, but are actually a deep, dark plum color.

Adding greens: Add a kelly-green flower (mini hydrangeas, solidaster) to make an arrangement brighter, a true green (most leaves: lemon leaves, fern, ruscus) to make it more neutral, or a dark green (dark green hydrangea, magnolia leaves) to make it more somber.

Unexpected color trios: Mix a hot color (e.g., hot pink) with a jewel tone (e.g., deep yellow) and a vibrant green or white for a nontraditional and unexpected look. Sample combinations include orange (*hot*), plum (*jewel tone*), and white or green; bright red (*hot*), burnt orange (*jewel tone*) and green; pink (*hot*), burgundy (*jewel tone*), and green.

IMPORTANT TERMS TO KNOW

There are countless terms used in floral design, but I have tried to use only the most basic ones. These are the terms used most often in my recipes:

- **Pavé:** A compact style of arrangement where the stems are cut low and the flower heads are placed tightly together.

- **Bunch:** Bunches are usually made up of 5 or 10 stems. Flowers that are thin-stemmed are mainly sold in bunches of 10 stems. Specialty, large, and tropical flowers are mainly sold in bunches of 5. Roses sold at a wholesale level are always sold in bunches of 25, but at a retailer they are usually sold by the dozen.

- **Rustic:** Natural-looking flowers, as if picked directly from a field.

- **Modern:** Structured designs with defined lines that create a distinct shape. A modern design should be architectural and tight.

- **Freehand:** An arrangement made without using a taped grid or floral foam to plan flower placement.

- **Domed:** This is when flowers are arranged to look like a dome: round, mounded, and circular.

- **Suspended:** A technique that balances stems or branches in the vase at an angle in the middle of the vase.

- **Submerged:** Flowers that are completely underwater, held down by either frog pins or rocks.

- **Collar:** Greenery or flowers placed around the entire rim of the vase, resembling a collar and giving the arrangement a polished look.

- **Spiraling:** A technique used to create a handheld bouquet by overlapping and angling stems, one by one, in the same direction.

- **Pulling through:** Flowers with really thin stems are hard to spiral into a bouquet because they break and flop over easily. And exact placements are difficult with spiraling. After you have spiraled a bouquet with the bigger/principal flowers (like hydrangeas or sunflowers), this technique (see sidebar) allows you to incorporate thinner-stemmed, secondary flowers (like clover or sweet peas) or greenery exactly where you want them.

DESIGN POINTERS

Here are some general guidelines to keep in mind as you arrange.

Insert flowers at an angle. Don't place flowers straight up and down in a vase unless you're creating rows (Roses and Grass on page 74) or a completely round shape (One-Size-Fits-All on page 71). Always add stems so that the blooms are leaning toward the outside of the arrangement. If you have a focal-point flower, one really special bloom you want to shine, then place it at an angle slightly off-center. You want the eye to travel over an arrangement, and placing a flower off-center makes it look more dynamic.

Measure before you cut. Take the first stem that you're going to use and hold it up next to the vase to estimate how short you should cut it. Always err on the longer side. Just like with hair or cloth, measure twice and cut once, because if you cut a flower too short, there's no going back. Place the stem inside the vase and see if it's the height you want. If it's not, cut off only about a quarter-inch to an inch more and then check it again by putting it in the vase. When you finally have the correct height, use that stem as a guide to cut the rest of the stems. This will save you a lot of time.

In many of my recipes, I say how much to trim each flower. For example, when I say "Cut the sunflowers to 5" to 6"," that means that the stem should be 5" to 6" long after cutting it (not including the flower or blooms at the top). Keep in mind that the initial stem size of flowers can vary, so while you might only need to cut an inch off one sunflower to get to 6 inches, you may have to cut almost a foot off another sunflower.

Don't agonize. Work quickly and don't worry about perfecting the design until the end. My advice is to always make the whole arrangement and then go back and fix, add, and tweak. This is especially true if you're making a bunch of arrangements for a party. Get the job done, then go back and finesse. You'll create better designs when you think less and don't deliberate over

HOW TO PULL THROUGH THINNER STEMS

To incorporate thinner-stemmed flowers into a bouquet when they aren't strong enough for spiraling, to exactly place exotic or expensive blooms that you want to show off, or to add greenery as an accent to the flowers, follow these steps.

1 Hold the bouquet in one hand, and, with the opposite hand, gently insert the thinner stem or greenery between the flowers already in the bouquet.

2 Loosen your grip on the bouquet slightly to allow the new stem to thread through to a point just below your hand.

3 Raise the bottom of the bouquet to eye level until you see the new stem poking through. Take the stem between your thumb and index finger and gently tug it down until the flower is at the height you want it.

every single stem along the way. When you add flowers quickly, the stems will also support each other, making it easier to balance them in an arrangement.

The shape of the vessel doesn't have to dictate the shape of the arrangement. Just because a vase is round or square doesn't mean the arrangement has to be the same shape. Add dimension by placing flowers facing outward at opposite angles. To do this, it's best to use flexible, pointy, long flowers such as Bells of Ireland, snapdragons, ruscus, and mini calla lilies. (See Everyday Hydrangeas on page 134 for an example.)

You don't always need more flowers to fill empty space. If you've used all the flowers you have, and there are still empty spaces in the arrangement, you'll need to bring the flowers in tighter and closer together. To do so, trim each stem shorter (I usually cut an inch at a time). Or you can even switch out your vase for a shorter one and cut down the flowers even more dramatically. Although it's kind of a pain, the good news is that you have the shape and pattern already done, so this part shouldn't take too long. The arrangement will look smaller since you're tightening it, but you don't have much choice if you've run out of flowers. If your design is meant to look more organic and rustic, you can get away with empty spaces in your arrangement.

Reject uniformity. If your arrangement ends up looking too structured instead of the organic, wildflower look that you wanted, then vary the height of your stems to create dimension. Pull some stems a little higher, or cut some a bit shorter than the rest—or do both. Make sure that the arrangement is asymmetrical, unless you are going for an intentionally symmetrical look;

different heights and shapes of flowers will make it look more natural.

Consider texture. If you want to create more texture in arrangements, the best thing to do is to mix shapes, using a variety of round and pointy flowers and leaves. If you want something more elegant, you should stick to one shape, such as all round blooms.

Cluster colors. Putting only one bright-colored flower in one spot of an arrangement makes that flower look sort of puny, and the color gets lost in the overall mix. Grouping a few of the same type of flowers together here and there gives them more impact in your arrangement.

Exert your influence. Flowers with stiff stems, such as dahlias or hydrangeas, can be very tricky to work with; sometimes they look as if they're going to tip over and fall out of the vase. If you find that a flower is stubbornly leaning too much one way, try twisting its stem 90 to 180 degrees so that the bloom is facing the opposite direction and then prop it against another flower in order to keep it in place. Be careful not to snap the bloom off the stem.

Don't be afraid to trim. Say you like where a multi-bloom flower is positioned within an arrangement, but one of its many blooms is hanging too low. In this case, use your scissors to cut one or more of the blooms off the stem. Save the small pieces you've cut off and add them in along the edge of the arrangement or put them in a small bud vase. Just be sure each tiny stem is in water.

You can trim from the top, too. When flowers are too tall for an arrangement, our instinct is to cut the stems from the bottom, but you *can* cut from the top, too. This approach can be useful when arranging snapdragons or stocks.

Cut a stem in half to double your flowers. [a] If you're arranging flowers in a short vase, there are some long-stemmed flowers you can cut in half to get more bang for your buck. Say you have a stem where flowers grow all the way up it, such as Bells of Ireland or dendrobium orchids. If you cut the stem in half immediately above one of the blooms—so that the cut is covered by the

nearest bloom or leaves—you now have two flowered stalks instead of one. Remove a few of the bottom blooms to elongate the new stem. (See photo on page 35.)

Work with odd numbers. Called the "rule of odds" in design, the idea is that our eyes naturally pull together items in pairs, so when there are odd numbers, arrangements look more dynamic and interesting. It's easy to do: Just use five tulips instead of four, or put three small bud vases on your mantel instead of two.

Keep leaves on the main stem. [b] If you place a single leaf into an arrangement, it will die within an hour; all leaves must be attached to the main stem of a flower. This is true for all leaves, including those of hydrangeas. If hydrangea stems are really long, cut the stem right above where the leaf is attached to the main stem, and place the cuttings aside in a bucket filled with a few inches of water so you can use these stems later on.

Turn the arrangement. Make sure to rotate your arrangement about halfway through arranging, to make sure the flowers are placed evenly throughout, or else you might end up with an unintentionally one-sided arrangement. For large arrangements, step back every now and then to see how your creation is coming along.

Fine-tune at the end. After the arrangement is finished, turn it around so you can view it from all angles. Pull up any flowers that have fallen down in the arranging process or that need to be angled more.

Use your leftovers. Have any discards, extras, snapped stems, or small blooms you couldn't use in your arrangement? Don't toss them out just yet. These leftovers are great to use for gifts, or to experiment with. Glass votives, espresso cups, wine or beer bottles, mason jars, and empty cans are all fun vessels in which to display leftover flowers.

3

SPIRALED
BOUQUETS

Spiraling is how you make a basic, round, tied bouquet. You can make a rustic-looking spiraled bouquet of wildflowers, a tiny posy of roses, or the classic dome shape seen in professional arrangements and wedding bouquets. They're all made using the spiraling technique. Out of all the approaches in the book, this one may require the most practice and patience. But once you master it, you'll be able to quickly whip up polished-looking bouquets in no time.

Whenever you spiral, keep in mind that speed is key. It's so much easier to work faster, because then the flowers support each other. You can go back and adjust at the end. If you add flowers really slowly, they'll start to push each other out, ruining the mounded effect.

GROCERY STORE SPIRAL

Easy, charming, and filled with blooms that you can grab at the grocery when you're shopping for dinner, this bouquet is a good way to practice spiraling—and to create a pretty arrangement for a friend or your coffee table. For this bouquet, buy whatever two different types of nicer-quality flowers appeal to you at the store, along with one bunch of filler flowers or greens. And if you get stuck later on in the book when spiraling, just refer back to this bouquet. This simple spiral provides the basic how-to steps for the technique.

(photographs continue on next page)

PREP TIME: 10 minutes   **COOK TIME:** 15 minutes   **SEASON:** Year round   **DIFFICULTY:** 2   **COST:** $–$$

INGREDIENTS

1 bunch of premium flowers (e.g., sunflowers, roses, tulips, dahlias, snapdragons)

1 bunch of another type of premium flower

1 bunch of filler flowers (e.g., alstroemeria, statice, mums, waxflower) or greenery

Something to bind the bouquet: thick green floral tape, clear elastic ponytail holder, piece of raffia, or whatever else you want to use

Small cylinder vase

DESIGN TIP: The closer to the blooms you bind the bouquet, the tighter-looking your bouquet will be. For a tight bouquet, wrap the floral tape or other binding material high on the stem, just under the blooms. If you're working with wildflowers and want a looser, more rustic bouquet, then wrap more toward the middle of the stems so that the flowers fan out. Experiment to see what you like best.

1 Prep all the flowers, then lay them out in 3 separate piles, divided by flower type.

2 Cut a piece of thick green floral tape 6" to 8" long (if using to bind the bouquet) and set it aside, within arm's reach.

3 Touch the tips of your thumb and index and middle fingers together to make a small circle. This is the holder for your flowers as you spiral. [a] Choose one premium flower and place it in the crook of your hand, so that the stem rests between your thumb and index finger about a third of the way down the stem.

4 Take the second type of premium flower and place it over the first flower, so that the stems meet in an X shape about a quarter of the way down. [b]

5 Add a stem of the greenery or filler flower to your fledgling bouquet, so that all 3 stems cross one another a third of the way down. Avoid clenching the stems; a stiff grip squishes the stems and stacks the flowers side by side instead of overlapping them in a spiral. [c]

6 Rotate the bouquet one quarter-turn to one half-turn. Add 3 more flowers—one of each type, one at a time. Cross their stems slightly closer up to their blooms than you crossed the previous 3 flowers. [d] This will position the blooms slightly lower than the first group, and begin to create the dome shape.

7 Continue adding in one type of each flower until all of the flowers are used or it looks full and is the size you want. After every turn or two of the bouquet, hold out the bouquet and look at its shape so far. Your goal is for the flowers at the center to be highest and for the bouquet to gradually and evenly slope down on all sides. If you need to adjust any flowers, loosen your grip ever so slightly and gently raise or lower blooms one at a time into the correct position. [e]

8 Once you have used all the ingredients and you have a pleasing, even dome shape, secure the bouquet by tightly wrapping the stems with your binding material of choice where you have been holding them. [f]

9 Measure the bouquet against the vase. You want the bottom of the outer blooms of the bouquet to rest on the vase rim. Cut the stems straight across and place the bouquet in the vase filled halfway with water.

(continued from prior page)

HOW TO MAKE A PROFESSIONAL-LOOKING WRAPPED BOUQUET

Remember when I said that in my first job, an associate taught me an easy way to professionally wrap flat bouquets without getting the tissue paper wet? Here's that trick.

1 Place a piece of tissue paper (green or white works with nearly any color combo) in between two sheets of cellophane to prevent water from leaking through. [a]

2 Starting from the top corner of the paper, alternate each type of flower, stacking 3 to 5 stems slightly on top of each other, until all the stems are used. Gather the

sides of the cellophane around the stems and staple in the center.

3 Tie a ribbon around the bouquet to cover the staple, then pull back the cellophane to show off the flowers. [b–c]

AUDREY'S ROSES

This bouquet is like one of my favorite actresses, Audrey Hepburn: classic, simple, and timeless. It would be ideal as a gift for a special occasion or for Valentine's Day. It's also a good example of a perfectly round spiral bouquet—with the ti leaf giving it a tiny nontraditional twist.

I like to practice spiraling with roses because their round shape and sturdy stems make it easy to get a dome look. The reason we overlap all of the stems in the same direction is that otherwise, opposite-facing stems might snap or break the other stems when the bouquet is secured—or at the very least, the stems wouldn't be smooth and symmetrical when secured under a ribbon.

INGREDIENTS

1 bunch of red roses (18 to 25 stems, depending on size of the rose)

1 ti leaf

Thick green floral tape

Corsage pins, wired twine, or stapler

Small cylinder vase

1 Prep the roses.

2 Force open the roses slightly (see page 15 for how to do this) so that the bouquet looks nice, full, and round.

3 Spiral the roses to form a bouquet, pulling up and adjusting any roses that slip down as you spiral to create a perfect dome.

4 Secure the bouquet with floral tape.

5 Cut off the top 6" to 8" of the ti leaf, then wrap it around the bouquet to cover the floral tape.

6 Secure the ti leaf. You can do this by wrapping wired twine around it or using a corsage pin to hold it in place. (If all else fails, staple it.)

7 Cut the stems to about 7" to 8" long. Place the bouquet in the vase filled halfway with water.

DESIGN TIP: Instead of a ti leaf, you could also wrap something sentimental around the bouquet. A bandanna, a necktie, or some pieces of a vintage dress that you pin with a sparkly brooch—the possibilities are endless.

SPIRALING ROSES

LIGHT AND LOVELY

This bouquet is light, fresh, and lovely—perfect for a summer garden party, baby shower, or wedding. Thin-stemmed flowers, such as sweet peas, give any bouquet or arrangement a delicate and whimsical look. But their stems make it hard to spiral them with thicker-stemmed flowers, since they bend easily. That's why pulling through (a technique described on page 39) works so well for these flowers. Hydrangeas spiral easily and provide a natural webbing through which to pull through the sweet peas and tuberose, letting you place them exactly where you want them in the bouquet.

PREP TIME: **10 minutes**   COOK TIME: **15 minutes**   SEASON: **Spring/Summer**   DIFFICULTY: **2**   COST: **$$–$$$**

INGREDIENTS

3 to 5 stems of white hydrangea

1 bunch of tuberose (or a few stems)

1 bunch of pink sweet peas (could substitute ranunculus or freesia)

Optional: dusty miller or seeded / silver dollar eucalyptus

Thick green floral tape, rubber band, or satin ribbon and corsage pin

Medium cylinder vase

CARE TIP: Tuberose blooms are very fragrant flowers. Fresh ones will have closed buds along the stem that open up into small white flowers. If they're closed, you can force open some of the buds by gently pinching the center and then pulling back the outer petals slightly.

1 Prep the hydrangea and tuberose. Cut the tuberose and hydrangea to about 10" to 12" long. The sweet peas don't need any prep, just a quick cut on a slant for the stem.

2 Spiral the hydrangea.

3 Pull through the tuberose, making sure they're evenly distributed.

4 Pull through the sweet peas [a], distributing them evenly throughout the bouquet. If you want, you can also pull through some eucalyptus or dusty miller.

5 Secure the bouquet with the thick green floral tape, a rubber band, or a satin ribbon secured with a corsage pin. Be careful not to snap the stems.

6 Place the bouquet in the vase filled halfway with water.

DESIGN TIP: For a looser, more natural look, vary the heights of the tuberose and sweet peas.

the flower chef

SUCCULENT BOUQUET

Anyone outdoorsy or who loves nature would appreciate this bouquet, since it's bursting with fantastic shapes and textures. But what really takes this arrangement over the top is the inclusion of succulents, which make this garden bouquet more unique. I love working with succulents, but the trouble with them is that they come in small containers and have very short stems or barely any stems at all. As a result, you need to create fake stems using floral wire and floral stem tape, so that they can be included in an arrangement. I'll show you how to do that for this earthy bouquet.

CARE TIP: One fun (and useful) fact about succulents is that they regenerate, meaning that after the rest of the flowers in this bouquet are dead, you can unwire the succulents and place a petal in soil to propagate.

PREP TIME: 25 minutes   **COOK TIME:** 20 minutes   **SEASON:** Fall/Winter/Spring   **DIFFICULTY:** 3   **COST:** $$$

INGREDIENTS

1 to 3 smaller 1" to 2" succulents

2 larger 3" to 4" succulents

1 bunch of orange ball dahlias (and/or any other kind of dahlia)

1 bunch of yellow and/or peach stock

1 bunch of white veronica or heather (similar in shape)

1 bunch of yellow ranunculus

A few stems of dusty miller

5 to 8 pieces of 18"-long 20-gauge straight stem wire

Floral stem tape

Thick green floral tape

Satin ribbon

Small cylinder vase

Optional: corsage pin

DESIGN TIP: Trim the wired stems just as you would any other flower stem. If they're too long, cut them to match the lengths of the other stems in the bouquet and then lightly push the wired stems toward the center of the bouquet to conceal them.

1 Lift the succulents out of their containers and remove the dirt and roots. Each large succulent will be left with a short stem, probably ½" to 1" long, and the smaller ones might have barely any stem at all.

2 For each of the smaller succulents, poke a piece of straight stem wire horizontally through what little stem they have, right below the base of the succulent. Thread it through until the succulent is centered on the wire. Bend both sides of the wire down so that it forms an upside-down U, or hairpin, with the succulent at the top of the upside-down U. This makes a stem for the succulent. [a]

3 For each of the larger succulents, you'll need to create a more substantial stem. To do so, insert a wire and make one upside-down U, or hairpin, as directed in step 2. Then rotate the flower one quarter-turn and insert a second wire perpendicular to the first wire, so that the two wires form a cross at the base of the succulent. You may have to use a little force to get the wires through the stem. Bend down the sides of the second wire, so that this also forms an upside-down U or hairpin.

4 Starting at the base of each of the succulents, wrap the floral stem tape around the wire stems you've created. [b] Twirl the stems with one hand and wrap with the other hand, overlapping the tape at a slant down the length of the stems. Pull the tape and squeeze the tape onto the stems as you wrap, since the tape is self-adhesive and will stick better that way. When you wrap to the bottom of the wire stems, tear off the tape. [c]

5 Prep all the flowers

6 Spiral the dahlias, stock, and veronica or heather.

7 Pull through the ranunculus and dusty miller so that they're evenly spaced throughout the bouquet.

8 Pull through the wired succulents, making sure that the large and small ones are evenly distributed. Because the succulent blooms may need a little extra support, try to position them so that they can gently rest on the non-succulent blooms.

9 Secure the bouquet with the thick green floral tape. Cover the tape with ribbon and secure with a corsage pin or tie the ribbon into a floppy bow.

10 Cut the stems (including the wired stems) to about 7" to 8" long. Place the bouquet in the vase filled halfway with water.

RETRO SURF BOUQUET

I live near the ocean, where surfers are always riding the waves and there's definitely a retro beach vibe. This bouquet, with its simple tropical look and laid-back feel, reminds me of my neighborhood. With only two ingredients (or three, if you add roses), this is the kind of arrangement I'd put on the table for a casual dinner with friends.

Since gladiolus is a flower with multiple blooms on its stem, I cut off the blooms for this bouquet and make a fake, wired stem for each bloom. Because gladioli are fairly fragile flowers, and they won't have any way to drink water through the fake stems, this bouquet really lasts only one night. If you decide to use longer-lasting blooms like orchids instead, the bouquet will last a couple days.

PREP TIME: 15 minutes   **COOK TIME:** 5 minutes   **SEASON:** Year round   **DIFFICULTY:** 2   **COST:** $–$$

INGREDIENTS

1 stem of a coral, pink, or peach gladiolus (or 5 to 6 blooms from a cymbidium orchid)

1 bunch of statice (pale yellow, lavender, or peach)

Optional: 1 bunch of small pale roses in any color (or 10 to 12 stems)

5 to 6 pieces of 18"-long 22-gauge straight stem wire, or enough to wire each gladiolus bloom

Floral stem tape

Thick green floral tape or rubber band

Satin ribbon

Corsage pin

Small cylinder vase

DESIGN TIP: If a flower breaks off the stem while you're arranging a bouquet (a snap is the worst sound a florist can hear!) and you're out of flowers, use this wiring method to save the broken flower and insert it in your arrangement.

1 Cut the blooms off the gladiolus stems. Wire the blooms and wrap with the floral stem tape, using the technique outlined in steps 2 and 4 from the Succulent Bouquet recipe (page 53). Set the wired stems aside.

2 Prep and spiral the statice (and roses, if using them).

3 Pull through however many gladioli you'd like. You may not need to use all of them. Even simply adding two close together can be really beautiful.

4 Secure the stems right underneath the blooms, with either the thick green floral tape or a rubber band. The bottom of the stems will spread out like a teepee.

5 Cover any exposed tape with ribbon and secure with a corsage pin or simply tie the ribbon in a bow.

6 Cut all the stems to about 7" to 8" long. Place the bouquet in the vase filled halfway with water.

DESIGN TIP: Try balancing the bouquet on the table for a vaseless arrangement by spreading out the stems like a teepee. You could add smaller arrangements or bud vases around it to create an entire tablescape.

MIDSUMMER NIGHT'S DREAMY

Dreamy, ethereal, and woodsy, this bouquet was inspired by *A Midsummer Night's Dream*. This would be beautiful for a nature-inspired wedding, or scattered on long tables for a candlelit spring dinner outside.

You can find the wood flowers and cotton in craft stores and floral supply stores, or you can order them online. Since they are reusable, these materials are both eco-friendly and economical.

PREP TIME: **10 minutes**   COOK TIME: **15 minutes**   SEASON: **Year round**   DIFFICULTY: **2**   COST: **$$**

INGREDIENTS

3 to 4 stems of mini green hydrangea

1 bunch of white lisianthus or ranunculus (or 3 to 5 stems)

2 to 3 stems of large wood flowers

1 bunch of small cream or brown balsa wood flowers

Optional: 1 bunch of scabiosa pods (or 3 to 5 stems); raw cotton (on stems, sold through wholesalers and some craft stores)

Thick green floral tape

Satin ribbon, twine, or burlap strips

Small cylinder vase

1 Prep the mini hydrangea. Prep the lisianthus by cutting off any secondary stems from the lisianthus so that a single stem has only a single bloom. Set the secondary stems aside.

2 Spiral the mini hydrangea to create the base of the bouquet.

3 Pull through the larger wood flowers and lisianthus evenly throughout the bouquet, turning the bouquet as you go to make sure the flowers are balanced.

4 Grouping a few stems of the scabiosa pods or raw cotton stems (if using) and balsa wood flowers together, position them next to the lisianthus and wood flowers and pull them through, evenly distributing them throughout the bouquet.

5 Using the secondary stems you cut off the lisianthus, pull them through; the greenery on these stems will break up the whites and browns of the rest of the bouquet.

6 Secure the bouquet with green floral tape and wrap twine, burlap, or ribbon around it to cover it up, tying the ends in a knot.

7 Cut the stems to about 7" to 8" long. Place the bouquet in the vase filled halfway with water.

DESIGN TIP: You can use the ingredients in this recipe, along with lime-green reindeer moss or mood moss, to create a beautiful table runner. Use the Garland Flowers recipe (page 211).

TULIP SWIRL

This is a super-simple bouquet that lets you play with color. Tulips—available year round and in a ton of colors—are a perfect way to make any arrangement pop. Try shades of pinks and purples for a classic, lovely look, or make a rainbow-colored bouquet for a kids' birthday party or an event requiring a little pizzazz.

PREP TIME: 10 minutes   COOK TIME: 10 minutes   SEASON: Year round   DIFFICULTY: 1   Cost: $–$$

INGREDIENTS

2 to 3 bunches of tulips in shades of pink and purple (or other compatible colors)

Thick green floral tape, or satin ribbon and corsage pin

Small cylinder vase

DESIGN TIP: For a beachy look, use all white tulips and place shells at the bottom of the vase.

1 Prep the tulips.

2 Spiral the tulips, alternating by color.

3 Secure midway down the stems with thick green floral tape or the ribbon and corsage pin. Cut off the bottom inch of the stems straight across. Place the bouquet in the vase filled halfway with water.

DESIGN TIP: Sometimes it's nice to make the stems look pretty as well. To do this, first secure the stems right under the blooms. Then hold the bouquet in one hand and twist the bottom of the stems counterclockwise with your other hand. Place the twisted stems inside the vase. Easy!

LUSH ROMANTIC BOUQUET

The full blooms of this bouquet couldn't be any more romantic, and the heady scent of the garden roses takes it over the top. Though I've suggested that you use a variety of pinks here, use all pale pinks to make the bouquet softer and more romantic. This would be gorgeous for a garden wedding, or to give to someone you love.

PREP TIME: 15 minutes   **COOK TIME:** 20 minutes   **SEASON:** Winter/Spring   **DIFFICULTY:** 2   **COST:** $$$$

INGREDIENTS

1 bunch of hot pink roses (or 12 to 16 stems)

1 bunch of coral and/or hot pink peonies

1 bunch of pink garden roses (or 5 to 6 stems)

1 bunch of ruscus or lemon leaves

Thick green floral tape

Pink satin ribbon or trim of your choice (e.g., lace, fabric)

Corsage pin or hot glue gun

Small cylinder vase

DESIGN TIP: If you're giving this bouquet as a gift, you want the blooms to be at least halfway open. If the bouquet is for a wedding, the blooms should be fully open.

1 Prep all the flowers, cutting the stems to 8" to 9" long, then separate them by type.

2 Cut 4 to 5 stems of the ruscus or lemon leaves to the same length as the flowers. Strip the leaves from the bottom two-thirds of each lemon leaf or ruscus.

3 Beginning with the regular roses, spiral all of the flowers, alternating the types until you have a nice, full, round bouquet.

4 Position the greens evenly throughout the bouquet and pull them through.

5 Secure the bouquet with the green floral tape. Cut all the stems to about 7" to 8" long.

6 Cover the tape by wrapping ribbon or trim around it. Secure with either hot glue or a corsage pin.

7 Place the bouquet in the vase filled halfway with water.

DESIGN TIP: After you've finished spiraling this bouquet, some of the blooms will be at various heights. The effect is a more natural, just-picked look with dimension and texture. If you prefer a smooth sphere shape (as shown on page 58), pull up the flowers that have sunk down a bit, so that all the flowers are even and the tips of the leaves are just poking out.

MODERN MINIMALIST BOUQUET

Green and yellow is one of my absolute favorite color combinations. Elegant and minimalist, this arrangement could be used for a wide variety of occasions, including a simple pick-me-up gift for a friend or to put on the table at a summer luncheon.

You could place this bouquet in a pitcher or a charming ceramic vase. I also like showcasing this bouquet in a vase with shells or white rocks.

PREP TIME: 20 minutes   COOK TIME: 15 minutes   SEASON: Year round   DIFFICULTY: 3   COST: $$$–$$$$

INGREDIENTS

1 stem of green and/or yellow cymbidium orchid

3 to 4 stems of mini green hydrangea

1 bunch of white and/or yellow mini calla lilies

Optional: 6 to 8 stems of white roses

5 to 6 pieces of 18"-long 22-gauge straight stem wire

Floral stem tape

Thick green floral tape

White or green satin ribbon

Corsage pin

Small vase

1 Cut 5 to 6 blooms from the cymbidium stem. Wire and tape them to create fake stems, using the technique in steps 2 and 4 from Succulent Bouquet (page 53).

2 Prep the roses, if you're using them, along with the mini hydrangea and calla lilies.

3 If you're using roses, begin by spiraling them with the mini hydrangea. If not, begin by spiraling the mini hydrangea.

4 Pull through the calla lilies and orchids so they're evenly distributed throughout the bouquet. Continue adding in the flowers until it's full and round.

5 Secure the bouquet just beneath the flowers and cut the stems so that they're all about 10" long. Wrap with ribbon and secure using a corsage pin or by tying a bow.

6 Place the bouquet in the vase filled halfway with water.

WILDFLOWER MEADOW

Imagine a huge field of wildflowers, greens and pinks and yellows and oranges, all blowing in the wind. So lovely, right? This bouquet is meant to mimic that feeling of casual untamed beauty. Keeping this in mind, buy flowers that look as if you found them growing on the side of the road or in a meadow. Long, thin stems work best. Although you'll still use the spiral technique, the arrangement will look more organic because you'll be gathering the flowers farther from the base of the blooms, which allows them to fan out.

PREP TIME: 15 minutes   COOK TIME: 20 minutes   SEASON: Year round   DIFFICULTY: 2   COST: $$$

INGREDIENTS

1 bunch of orange or pink snapdragons

1 bunch of yellow snapdragons

1 bunch of waxflower

1 bunch of Bells of Ireland

1 bunch of eucalyptus

Thick green floral tape

Medium vase or pitcher

DESIGN TIP: For a jewel-toned variation on this bouquet, use deep purple, red, and yellow flowers, such as coxcomb, lisianthus, and larkspur.

1 Prep the flowers and eucalyptus and cut all the stems to about 20" to 24" long.

2 Separate the flowers by type. Spiral all of the flowers, alternating the types as you go. Grip the stems lower than you would for other spiral bouquets—in this case, about halfway down the stems.

3 Secure the bouquet with tape at the same point where you've been gripping the stems.

4 Measure the bouquet against your vase and cut it to the height you want.

5 Place the bouquet in the vase filled halfway with water and fan out the flowers so the arrangement has a wild, just-picked feel.

DESIGN TIP: As a general rule, the height of the flowers should be no more than twice the height of the vase. I don't hold steadfast to this rule, though. You can make a pavé-style arrangement in a medium vase or an organic tall style in a low vase.

CALIFORNIA VINTAGE

With their slightly faded tones and sunny warmth, the colors in this small bouquet remind me of a vintage postcard or the California landscape. Plus, I love the color combination of yellow, orange, and green. This is a spark of sunshine for a cold winter day, perfect to give as a gift or to perk up your living room.

Note that though the recipe calls for flowers by the bunch, a few stems of each would be just fine, making it almost look like a sweet posy.

PREP TIME: **15 minutes**   COOK TIME: **10 minutes**   SEASON: **Fall/Winter/Spring**   DIFFICULTY: **2**   COST: **$$$**

INGREDIENTS

1 bunch of yellow stock (or 4 to 5 stems)

1 bunch of yellow ranunculus (or 4 to 5 stems)

1 bunch of yellow freesia (or 4 to 5 stems)

1 bunch of white or green 'Safari Sunset,' also called 'Safari Goldstrike (or 4 to 5 stems)

1 bunch of solidaster (or 4 to 5 stems)

1 vine of kumquats (a branch is about 2' to 3' long)

Thick green floral tape

Ribbon, raffia, or twine

Small cylinder vase

1 Prep the flowers, in this case stripping the leaves off the bottom half of each stem. Separate the flowers by type.

2 Spiral the flowers, alternating by type. Since you want a wilder, more natural look here, vary the heights of the flowers as you add them into the bouquet.

3 Cut the kumquat vine into 3 sections, each about 8" to 10" long, depending on the height of your other flowers. Pull the kumquat vines through the bouquet so they're evenly distributed. Position them at different heights.

4 Secure the bouquet just under the blooms with thick green floral tape.

5 Hide the tape by tying a bow with ribbon, raffia, or twine.

6 Cut the stems to about 7" to 8" long. Place the bouquet in the vase filled halfway with water.

CARE TIP: As you get more advanced, you'll be able to remove leaves using only one hand—just like chefs crack eggs using one hand—when adding in stems to a bouquet.

SEPIA FLOWERS

I really cherish family and I love looking at vintage photographs of my grandparents. In one sepia-toned photo, my grandmother is carrying a small Bible adorned with cymbidium orchids and ribbon. This dreamy, old-fashioned bouquet was inspired by that photo, and by imagining my grandmother on her wedding day so many decades ago.

This bouquet is slightly cascading, which means that some of the flowers are intentionally drooping down on one side. The effect can be achieved by using long flowers such as orchids, or with greenery such as seeded eucalyptus, which is what I use here.

PREP TIME: 25 minutes   **COOK TIME:** 25 minutes   **SEASON:** Fall/Winter/Spring   **DIFFICULTY:** 3   **COST:** $$$$

INGREDIENTS

1 stem of brown cymbidium orchid

1 stem of pink cymbidium orchid

1 bunch of white or pink lisianthus

1 bunch of chocolate cosmos

1 bunch of plum dahlias

1 bunch of cream spray roses

1 bunch of seeded eucalyptus

4 to 5 pieces of 18"-long 22-gauge straight stem wire

Floral stem tape

Thick green floral tape

Cream or brown satin ribbon or lace

Bronze or gold vase, or small round glass vase

1 Prep the flowers, then separate them into groups by type. Set aside any flowers that are bending downward.

2 Cut 4 to 5 blooms from each cymbidium stem. Wire and tape them to create fake stems, using the technique in steps 2 and 4 from Succulent Bouquet (page 53).

3 Spiral the lisianthus, cosmos, dahlias, and roses together, alternating types as you go.

4 Once most of the flowers are spiraled in (you won't use all of the flowers, just enough so that the bouquet looks full and round), pull through the wired orchids so that they're evenly distributed.

5 Take a few of the bended stems you set aside and add them to an outer edge of the bouquet, clustering them on one side. Make sure these flowers curve out and down, giving the arrangement a cascading look.

6 Add the eucalyptus to that same outer edge, pulling them out so the seeds and leaves cascade even more off that side.

7 Secure the bouquet with thick green floral tape and cut the stems to about 8" long.

8 Wrap ribbon or lace around the tape and tie it in a bow, leaving the ends of the ribbon trailing down.

9 Fill the vase halfway with water. Place the bouquet in the vase at an angle, so that the flowers cascade over the side.

DESIGN TIP: As a fun alternative to lace, soak cheesecloth (you can buy it at the grocery store) in weak black tea to create an antique look and use it as ribbon.

4

FLORAL FOAM

Floral foam is a synthetic material that is sold in the shape of green bricks by floral supply stores, craft stores, and florists. Lightweight and water absorbent, it is great to use in containers that you aren't able to fill with water (like baskets or shallow bowls), since flower stems can drink water from the foam. It's also a perfect tool to use in arrangements where you want to insert flowers in precise places, such as a very elaborate holiday centerpiece, since the foam acts like an anchor and keeps stems exactly where you've inserted them. But beware—it's crumbly and messy, especially when it's dry, so cut it only after you've fully soaked it in water. Be sure to buy floral foam intended for fresh flowers, not artificial flowers.

One timing note: It's important to prep your foam the day of or the day before you plan on making your arrangement. Otherwise, the foam will start to crumble if left in a bucket of water for too long and will be harder to work with.

Because the foam is the main source of water for your arrangement, it's important that it stays wet. After you have finished arranging, place your finger on top of the foam to check if it is thoroughly wet. If it isn't, pour a half cup or so of water. Flowers should last as long in foam as they do in water. Add water to the foam if it begins to feel dry after a day or two.

In this chapter, each recipe calls for an opaque vessel in order to hide the foam. Note that when you use foam in containers that are porous, like wooden boxes, you will need to line the container, covering its bottom and sides with a folded trash bag, cellophane, or specialty foil covered in plastic. Place the liner inside, lay the foam down, and then cut off the excess plastic or push it down in the vase so that you can't see it once you add the flowers. Some wood boxes come already fitted with removable plastic liners. In this case, you don't need to worry about making your own liner. In chapter 6, we'll get more advanced by lining transparent vases with ti leaves.

HOW TO PREP AND INSTALL FLORAL FOAM FOR YOUR ARRANGEMENT

1 Soak the floral foam in water. Fill a sink or bucket with cool water, then place a foam brick on top of the water's surface. The foam will slowly submerge as it absorbs water. If the foam has holes on one side (often found in "instant foam," which has a quicker absorption time), place the holes facedown on the water. Let it stay in the water for 10 to 20 minutes to make sure it's completely soaked. You can cut a small slice off the end, or cut it in half to test the center, to make sure the foam is full of water; if it still has dry spots inside (they'll look lighter than the wet foam), soak it for longer.

2 Using a butter knife, chef's knife, or floral knife, cut the foam brick to about the width and length of the top of whatever vase or dish you're using to hold the foam. Use any small leftover pieces to fill inside the sides of the vase so that it's packed tightly.

3 Cut any foam that is sticking out of the vase to make it flush with the top of the vase so that you don't see any foam when the arrangement is done. Sometimes, when I'm using a very tall vase, I'll stack two bricks vertically on top of each other, and the foam still won't reach the top. That's fine. Just make sure that whatever you do, all of your flower stems can reach the foam—otherwise, they won't have access to water.

CARE TIP: Don't press the foam down with your hand to get it to better fit in the vase. Doing that compresses the foam and makes it harder to insert stems. Instead, just trim as needed to get the right fit.

ONE-SIZE-FITS-ALL

Gender-neutral, easy to scale up or down, and streamlined, this is the perfect one-size-fits-all pavé arrangement that is both traditional and modern. If you want to send a thank-you to a work colleague or give a friend flowers for their desk or make a gift for someone you don't know too well, this arrangement would be lovely. Straightforward and simple, it's good for everyone.

This design should end up in a dome shape, with the roses at the center higher than those at the edges. I first tried making this arrangement without any foam or floral tape, and no matter what I did, I couldn't make a dome because the flowers kept flopping over to one side.

PREP TIME: **5 minutes** COOK TIME: **15 minutes** SEASON: **Year round** DIFFICULTY: **2** COST: **$–$$**

INGREDIENTS

1 bunch of yellow roses
(or 15 stems)

1 block of floral foam

5" to 6" ceramic or opaque
square or round vase

1 Soak the floral foam, then trim it to fit the vase and place it snugly inside.

2 Prep the roses and cut all the stems to about 6" long. Force open the roses by blowing on them in the center and quickly pushing out the outer petals.

3 Take the first stem and place it directly in the center of the foam, about 5" high. Take 4 more stems and place them in each corner at an angle so that the rose heads rest on the edge of the vase. You may need to cut the stems shorter to get the roses to sit lower.

4 Place the next 4 roses on each side of the vase, between the corner roses.

5 Add in 6 stems of roses evenly around the center stem.

6 The arrangement should resemble a dome. If there's space in between the roses, push the stems farther into the foam, or remove each stem one at a time, trim down ½", and reinsert, to bring all of the blooms closer together.

DESIGN TIP: For extra pizzazz, you can create a collar made out of Bells of Ireland. First, insert a couple stems of the bells deep into the foam, a few inches apart from each other. Second, wrap the stems around the rim of the vase. Tuck the end of the bells into the vase to secure so that they create a collar around the entire circumference of the vase. Note: Make sure that the stems of bells you choose have a curve to them so that they bend around the vase without snapping.

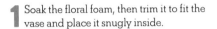

THINKING OF YOU

Sometimes you just want to cheer up someone with some flowers. Maybe your friend has just broken up with his or her significant other, or maybe your sibling recently changed jobs. Or maybe you haven't seen a cousin for a long time. With its quietly cheerful colors and the bright splash of green, this is a sweet arrangement to send a person "just because." In an unexpected combination, the pop of true red makes the other colors look brighter.

Note that the recipe calls for an 8" ceramic vase. If you're using a smaller (4" to 6") or a larger (10") vase, decrease or increase the recipe by a third or a half.

PREP TIME: 15 minutes   COOK TIME: 15 minutes   SEASON: Year round   DIFFICULTY: 1   COST: $$$

INGREDIENTS

4 to 5 stems of white or sage hydrangea

1 bunch of red roses (or 6 to 8 stems)

10 to 12 stems of mixed-color roses (peach, orange, yellow, pink)

1 bunch of pink sweet peas

1 block of floral foam

8" square green ceramic vase

DESIGN TIP: Placing the stems of other flowers through the hydrangea and into the foam creates an upscale look. This is true for all hydrangea arrangements. Only when I'm creating a more rustic design will I place flowers between the hydrangea stems, which encourages the hydrangea to spread out a bit.

1 Soak the floral foam, then trim it to fit the vase and place it snugly inside.

2 Prep the flowers and cut all the stems to about 8" long.

3 Place the first hydrangea diagonally into the foam at one corner, facing outward. The head of the flower should rest on both the top of the foam and the vase, so trim these stems as needed.

4 Repeat with the remaining hydrangeas, placing them in opposite corners. If you only have room to use 3 hydrangeas, position them in a triangle, rather than a square. Just make sure they cover the entire surface of the foam.

5 Insert the roses in random clusters of 2 to 3 stems throughout the foam.

6 To ensure even distribution, rotate the vase in quarter-turn intervals as you go.

7 Add in the sweet peas as accents, evenly distributed throughout the arrangement.

DESIGN TIP: Sometimes the foam will seem fully covered when you look at the arrangement from above, but be sure to bend down and look at it from eye level. This is especially important for long and low centerpieces where guests will be looking at arrangements from their seats.

floral foam

ROSES AND GRASS

This is a fun twist on a traditional rose arrangement. Fast, easy to replicate, and inexpensive to make, the modern shape is softened by the muted palette. You could easily customize this, making it with your mom's favorite roses for Mother's Day, or as a beautiful hostess gift in seasonal hues if you're invited to a party.

The moss in the arrangement covers the exposed foam and, combined with the bear grass, adds a subtle earthiness to the stark rows of roses. I use green floral wire to secure the moss to the foam. There are premade U-shaped hairpins available at floral supply and craft stores, but I usually use straight wire that I have on hand. The ingredients below are adjusted to whatever size arrangement you'd like to make.

PREP TIME: 10 minutes COOK TIME: 15 minutes SEASON: Year round DIFFICULTY: 1 COST: $$–$$$

INGREDIENTS

SMALL
12 purple roses
8 white roses
6" wood box

MEDIUM
15 purple roses
10 white roses
8" wood box

LARGE
21 purple roses
14 white roses
10" wood box

1 bunch of bear grass

Sheet moss (or any moss will do)

Plastic liner for your container

1 to 2 blocks of floral foam

1 piece of 18"-long 20- to 22-gauge straight stem wire

DESIGN TIP: The medium-sized recipe calls for 15 purple roses and 10 white roses. This is where buying gets tricky. Generally a single rose will cost $2 to $3, so it's better to buy a dozen or two at $10 to $12 each, or a wholesale bunch (25 stems) for $15 to $20, and have leftovers to place around your home.

1 If the wood box doesn't have a liner, place a small trash bag or piece of cellophane inside so that it covers the bottom and sides.

2 Soak the floral foam, then cut the foam to fit the box and place it snugly inside. Trim or tuck in any of the liner that is poking out from the box.

3 Trim the roses to about 4" long and remove any remaining leaves. (Since you will be cutting the roses short, there is no need to spend time cleaning the stems prior to cutting them.)

4 Make a row of purple roses along the top of the box. Starting ½" in from the edge of the vase, place each rose into the foam pointing straight up so that the bloom rests ½" above the foam. Create a uniform row across the top of the vase, with minimal space between the blooms so that the foam is hidden. Leave ½" of foam exposed around the entire perimeter of the vase.

5 Using white roses, begin a new row directly below the one you just formed. Continue with rows of alternating colors of roses, until you complete the last row along the bottom edge of the box.

6 Cut 4 blades of bear grass straight across at the top and bottom so that each blade measures 4" to 5" tall. Insert the cluster of blades into the foam between the roses. The blades should stand an inch or so above the roses once fully inserted. Repeat in 4 to 6 other areas of the arrangement, so that the bear grass is evenly dispersed throughout the box.

7 Take a piece of moss and stretch it gently. Cover all the exposed foam with moss. You'll probably have to cut the moss into smaller pieces to get it to fit around the roses.

8 To secure the moss into the foam, create a small hairpin or upside-down U shape of wire. To do this, cut a 2"-long piece of wire and bend it in half so that it looks like a hairpin. Insert the wire into the moss and through the foam, deep enough so that the moss covers the wire. Continue to add hairpins around the perimeter of the arrangement until the moss is secure.

ROSES AND PODS

Similar to Roses and Grass, this is super-simple but very elegant. For the winter holidays, you can use red roses with green berries, or for spring, try bright yellow roses with lime-green hypericum.

INGREDIENTS

1 bunch of white roses

1 bunch of seasonal green pods or berries, such as berzelia or hypericum

1 block of floral foam

8" square white ceramic or opaque vase

1 Soak the floral foam, then trim the foam to fit the vase and place it snugly inside.

2 Cut all the roses to about 4" long.

3 Make a row of roses along the top of the box, as described in step 4 of Roses and Grass (page 74).

4 Continue making uniform rows of roses until you reach the bottom edge of the box. Try to leave a 1" perimeter of exposed foam around the entire edge of the box.

5 Cut the branches of the pods or berry stems to about 1" long. Place the stems into the exposed foam, completely filling all of the space between the roses and the edge of the vase.

CARE TIP: Since white flowers can quickly turn brownish, especially around the edges of petals, spraying your arrangement with floral preservative can help it look fresh longer.

JAMAICAN DELIGHT

I like to say that this is the arrangement that started it all. Before I opened my business, my boyfriend at the time loved anything having to do with Jamaica, so I played around with a design that used flowers in the colors of the country's flag. Surprisingly, though it was my first-ever arrangement, it's become one of my most popular designs for men and women alike. Bright, happy, and dynamic, it's an instant visual pick-me-up on even the cloudiest of days.

With this recipe you can be flexible with the number of stems of each type of flower you use.

PREP TIME: 15 minutes   **COOK TIME: 25 minutes**   **SEASON: Year round**   **DIFFICULTY: 2**   **COST: $$$**

INGREDIENTS

1 bunch of yellow/orange roses (12 to 16 stems)

1 bunch of Bells of Ireland

1 bunch of pink or orange snapdragons

1 bunch of yellow ranunculus

1 to 2 blocks of floral foam

8" square ceramic or opaque vase

1 Soak the floral foam, then trim the foam to fit the vase and place it snugly inside.

2 Prep the roses. For this arrangement, you can leave some of the topmost leaves on the stems since they will blend into the arrangement.

3 Cut 5 to 6 roses to 10" long and place them evenly throughout the foam, angled away from the center of the vase.

4 Cut another 5 to 6 roses to 8" long and place them evenly in between the other roses.

5 Cut the remaining roses to 6" long and place them toward the edge of the vase. At each corner of the vase, insert a stem or two as far as they can go so that the rose heads touch the rim of the vase.

6 Prep and cut the Bells of Ireland to 8" to 10" long.

7 Place the stems of bells throughout the foam, inserting each on an angle. They should all point in different directions, mostly outward.

8 Cut the snapdragons to 8" to 10" long and strip off some of the little leaves. It's not important to have them perfectly clean since you'll only see the blooms. Place them evenly throughout the arrangement, turning it to make sure the flowers are evenly balanced. They should all be at varying heights.

9 Cut the ranunculus to 6" long. Add them toward the outside of the arrangement, where the yellow will pop. The stems are fragile, so take a bit more time and care with them, gently inserting them into the foam. If a stem bends, cut it shorter above the bend and insert it into the foam closer to the outside of the bouquet.

CARE TIP: If you're having a hard time getting thin stems into the foam, take a floral pick or rose stem and poke a hole into the foam, then insert the flower.

GEMSTONE CENTERPIECE

With an assortment of jewel tones and textures, this is a gorgeous arrangement for autumn and could easily inspire the design for a whole wedding or party. Can't you just picture tables covered with glimmering gold mercury candle holders, bottles of delicious red wine, and dark burgundy linens—with these flowers as the centerpieces? This is definitely a sophisticated, decadent arrangement for a special event.

To that end, you'll notice that there is no greenery here, just premium flowers, which creates the rich, dense look. The texture comes from the mixture of pointy and round flowers. Since it takes a lot of flowers to fill up a vase without any filler or greens, this is a more expensive arrangement than others. Note that we're adding flowers in order of their size, from the largest blooms to the smallest.

PREP TIME: 20 minutes   COOK TIME: 30 minutes   SEASON: Fall/Winter/Spring   DIFFICULTY: 2   COST: $$–$$$

INGREDIENTS

1 bunch of orange or yellow roses (or 12 to 16 stems)

1 bunch of dark plum / black mini calla lilies

1 bunch of yellow and / or plum ranunculus

Optional: billy balls and fiddleheads

1 block of floral foam

Pedestal vase (bronze, brown, gold) or metallic serving bowl

DESIGN TIP: Substitute dahlias and / or various types of mums for roses to create even more visual interest.

1 Soak the floral foam, then trim the foam to fit the vase or bowl and place it snugly inside.

2 Prep the flowers and cut all the stems to about 6" to 7" long.

3 Using the method from One-Size-Fits-All (page 71), form an outline of a dome shape with the roses.

4 Add in the calla lilies throughout, turning the arrangement to make sure the colors are evenly balanced.

5 Place the ranunculus evenly throughout the arrangement. You can poke holes in the foam when adding in ranunculus, too. The black mini callas and plum ranunculus will pop out the most, so place them strategically next to the orange and yellow flowers.

6 If using billy balls and fiddleheads, add them sparingly throughout the arrangement.

CARE TIP: You can make this arrangement up to 2 days before an event since these flowers are long-lasting.

QUIRKY COLLAGE

This arrangement, with its seemingly random elements, doesn't take itself too seriously and is quirky—a bit like me! Nothing in this design seems to go together, yet everything comes together perfectly. I picked colors and shapes that I like, and I just had fun with it. Try it sometime! Have a glass of wine, play with flowers, and see what happens.

It's very common to use a plastic dish for both rectangular and round arrangements. They are affordable and reusable, and they're good for a narrow space, like a mantel, counter, or long dining table. The flowers will naturally drape over the side and can be maneuvered to conceal any exposed plastic. You can create a longer centerpiece by extending the stems out from the dish. If you buy a 12" dish and extend it on both sides with longer flowers, your centerpiece can end up being 20" to 24" long.

PREP TIME: 10 minutes **COOK TIME:** 30 minutes **SEASON:** Spring/Summer/Fall **DIFFICULTY:** 2 **COST:** $$$

INGREDIENTS

8 to 10 stems of sage hydrangea

1 bunch of pink gerbera daisies

1 bunch of green amaranthus

1 bunch of pink coxcomb

3 stems of king protea

2 blocks of floral foam

14" plastic rectangle dish

CARE TIP: Every few days, touch the floral foam to see if it's getting dry. Add a half cup of water at a time to keep it wet.

1 Soak the floral foam, then place the blocks of foam next to each other in the dish.

2 Prep all the flowers.

3 Cut 2 stems of hydrangea to about 6" to 7" long, then stick one into the foam on each end of the dish, angled out and inserted a few inches deep so they're secure.

4 Cut the remaining 6 to 8 hydrangeas to about 4" to 5" long and insert them into the foam down the length of the container so that they cover the foam and the sides of the dish. Alternate the sides in which you're inserting them to create a zigzag pattern. If foam is visible when finished, remove the hydrangea with the biggest bloom, cut the bottom of the stem where the web of smaller stems meet, and break apart the hydrangea into many smaller pieces. Insert the smaller pieces in the empty spaces to hide the foam.

5 Insert the gerbera daisies into the foam so that they create a diagonal line that runs from one corner of the dish to the opposite one. It's best if the row is not perfectly straight and if it does not exactly bisect the arrangement. The row should look as if it's meandering. To create this almost-but-not-quite symmetrical look, start with one daisy slightly to the left or the right of the center of the dish, then add 2 to 3 at a time on each side until you reach each corner.

6 Cut the amaranthus to about 3" long and remove some of the leaves from the bottom half of the stems. Thread a few stems of amaranthus through the hydrangea and into the foam so that they drape over the sides. If they look too long once you've inserted them, remove the stem, trim it, and reinsert.

7 Cluster 2 to 3 stems of coxcomb next to each other in the front and back corners on opposite sides. They are narrow stems, so they need to be grouped for impact.

8 Insert the protea far enough into the foam so that only the flowers are visible, not the stems. Since these flowers are focal points in the arrangement, place one on either side, on opposite edges of the dish. Pair the third with one of the other two proteas, so that there are two on one side and one on the other.

9 Closely examine the arrangement at eye level. You don't want anyone to see the plastic dish; the hydrangeas and amaranthus should completely cover the lip of the dish. If, however, any part is still visible, tug the hydrangea stems out a bit and then use your hand to gently pull them downward to cover the offending spots. Avoid too much contact with the hydrangeas so that you don't wilt them with the warmth and oil of your hands.

STILL-LIFE CENTERPIECE

This arrangement reminds me of a still-life painting, because of the muted color palette and the addition of fruits and vegetables. Charming, with a dash of whimsy, this would be perfect as the centerpiece for a family gathering or holiday dinner.

Feel free to use up your older produce—just make sure it's not too soft, since you don't want it to turn to mush or rot. Add in the fruit last, using wood floral picks. A variety of flowers is good for this arrangement, especially wildflowers. Feel free to brighten up the palette with kiwis, apricots, and even limes.

PREP TIME: 15 minutes **COOK TIME:** 25 minutes **SEASON:** Spring/Summer/Fall **DIFFICULTY:** 3 **COST:** $$$–$$$$

INGREDIENTS

4 to 5 pieces of produce (artichokes, plums, kiwis)

1 bunch of white veronica or heather

1 to 2 bunches of stock (yellow, peach, pink, or white)

1 bunch of pink lisianthus or roses (10 to 12 stems)

1 bunch of pink, white, or peach dahlias

1 bunch of cream or green hypericum

1 to 2 blocks of floral foam (depending on bowl size)

Wooden green floral picks (or any wood picks such as kebab sticks)

Serving bowl

Optional: thick green floral tape

1 Soak the floral foam, then cut the foam so that it fits snugly in the bowl. If you're using a very low bowl and it seems like the foam is going to fall out, stretch multiple strips of the floral tape around the bowl and the foam, crisscrossing as you go so that the strips make a cross or a star shape over the top of the foam to hold it in (see the Branch Out recipe on page 100).

2 Cut or break the floral picks so that they are about 6" long. It's OK if the end is jagged; that will make it easier to pierce the fruit or vegetable. Insert the pointy end of one stick about an inch deep into a piece of produce; spearing the produce anywhere is fine, as long as it's secure. (Note: Artichokes are the exception and should be speared 2" deep directly into the stems.) Do this with each piece of fruit and vegetable you're using.

3 Prep the flowers and then separate them by type. You can keep some foliage at the top if you'd like.

4 Cut a few stems of veronica (or heather) and stock to about 8" to 10" long. Cut another few stems of the same types of flowers to about 4" to 5" long.

5 Using the veronica (or heather) and stock, form an asymmetrical V shape as the starting outline for the arrangement (see photo at right). Insert the taller veronica and stock, angled moderately outward, on the left side. Insert the shorter veronica and stock on the right side, angled outward almost horizontally. If possible, bend the shorter pieces a bit downward, being careful not to snap the stems. The arrangement should be asymmetrical overall.

6 A very open V shape will start to form. Cut a few stems of the lisianthus, or roses, to the same height as the taller veronica and place them nearby, following the rough outline that has developed. Cut a few stems of the lisianthus, or roses, to the same height as the shorter veronica and place them near those stems.

7 Cut the dahlias to about 6" to 8" long and place them evenly throughout the entire arrangement, some at the midway height between the taller and shorter flowers, creating a smooth, gradual line. You can place a taller stem toward the left side. Cut half at 8" and place at the top of the V, then cut half at 6" and put at the bottom of the V.

8 Add in the hypericum and evenly distribute throughout. The flowers don't have to be in a certain order or pattern; just make sure the colors are balanced.

9 Add in the rest of the stock and veronica to further define the V shape. Turn the vase and add flowers so that the arrangement looks full.

10 Add in the produce at the bottom half of the arrangement. Rotate the arrangement about one quarter-turn after each insertion to ensure that the fruit and vegetables are evenly distributed.

DESIGN TIP: Create a matching side arrangement with leftover flowers or simply fill a pretty smaller bowl with leftover produce.

PUTTING ON THE GLITZ

Add a little glitz and glamour to your flowers with this super-simple technique. Spray-painted and dyed flowers look chic any time of year, and I especially love to spray-paint greenery in a metallic shade. Pre-sprayed leaves are available at craft stores, but painting your own lets you get exactly the color and look you want.

You can use regular spray paint for foliage, but watch out for its toxic fumes (which is why it's best to do it outside or somewhere well ventilated). Because of this, I prefer to use special flower spray paint that you can buy online or from a floral supply or craft store. It dries within 10 minutes, doesn't smell as strong, and comes in every color.

You can use this technique for any season, using bright colors for fun flowers for a summer barbecue or a lovely muted pastel palette for a spring baby or bridal shower. This is a quick, inexpensive arrangement to make, and here I've gone with a sparkly gold and white winter theme that would be easy and special to give as a holiday gift or for a holiday party with friends.

PREP TIME: 15 minutes   COOK TIME: 10 minutes   SEASON: Year round   DIFFICULTY: 1   COST: $–$$

INGREDIENTS

1 bunch of baby's breath

4 to 5 stems of lemon leaves

7 to 8 stems of white spider mums

1 block of floral foam

Gold spray paint

6" to 8" round glass or gold (or spray-painted gold) vase

DESIGN TIP: Spray-paint pinecones silver or gold and place them around the base of the vase on the table or on a decorative plate. These pinecones can then be used year after year!

1 Soak the floral foam, then trim the foam to fit the vase and place it snugly inside. Trim the top of the foam so that it's even with the top of the vase.

2 Working outside, put a trash bag or newspaper under the lemon leaves and baby's breath and spray-paint the leaves and buds on both sides. Let them dry for 10 minutes. You'll be cutting the stems short for this arrangement, so there's no need to fully prep the flowers or greens beforehand.

3 Cut the lemon leaves to about 3" to 4" long, removing any leaves on the very bottom. Place the lemon leaves evenly throughout the foam.

4 Cut a few stems of the baby's breath about the same length as the lemon leaves. Insert them next to the lemon leaves, angling them out, so they stick out a bit on the sides.

5 Prep the mums and cut the stems to about 6" long. Ring the rim of the vase with 5 mums, evenly spaced. Put the other 2 to 3 mums in the center, set slightly asymmetrically, to fill out the arrangement. Angle all the flowers up and outward.

6 Fill in any holes or exposed foam with small bunches (a few stems) of baby's breath, cut short.

DESIGN TIP: Any flowers that you want to highlight should be added to the arrangement last, because they're the first flowers you want to see.

STRIPED CENTERPIECE

Always in style, stripes let you mix and match colors for a bold look that pops, or create subtle shades in the same hues. Whatever you do, stripes make it easy to play around with color and texture.

You can make this arrangement all year round with any in-season flowers. It's particularly good for Thanksgiving or any type of dinner party since it fits nicely on a long dining room table. Either a rectangular plastic dish or a rectangular wooden vase work as vessels. But keep in mind that if you're using a plastic dish, you'll need more flowers to cover the plastic sides.

PREP TIME: 10 minutes   COOK TIME: 20 minutes   SEASON: Year round   DIFFICULTY: 1   COST: $$$–$$$$

INGREDIENTS

12 to 15 stems (depending on size) of mini green hydrangea

2 bunches of marigolds, sunflowers, or any round orange/yellow seasonal flower

6 to 8 stems (depending on size) of white or green ornamental kale with stem

2 blocks of floral foam

12" to 16" wood rectangle vase with plastic liner

1 Soak the foam, then trim the foam to fit the vase and place it snugly inside.

2 Prep the flowers and cut all the stems to about 6" long.

3 Place one hydrangea directly into the center of the vase, inserting the stem a few inches deep into the foam.

4 Place 2 hydrangeas on either side of the first one, creating a row that stretches widthwise across the vase. (If the ends of the stems stick out of the foam, cut them shorter so the bottoms of the stems are in the foam. Otherwise, they can't drink any water.)

5 Using the same technique as with the hydrangea, create a new row to the right of the hydrangea with the marigolds or sunflowers.

6 To the right of the marigolds or sunflowers, create a row of kale.

7 To the right of the kale (and at the end of the vase), create a row of hydrangea, making sure the blooms drape over the end of the vase. You've now completed half of the arrangement.

8 Make the other half of the arrangement, creating these rows to the left of the center hydrangeas: first a row of kale, then a row of marigolds or sunflowers, and then a final row of hydrangeas to match the one at the opposite end of the vase.

DESIGN TIP: Mix and match the colors of this arrangement, and consider adding in pops of white or dark green flowers or leaves, depending on the season and occasion.

the flower chef

CANDLELIT CENTERPIECE

When you're a florist, you're always asked to bring the flowers when you're invited to a friend's house for the holidays. One year, I was invited to a Thanksgiving dinner and hadn't planned ahead of time what to make. So I headed to the grocery store to find inspiration. Grabbing three premade bouquets of flowers in warm colors, I spotted kumquat branches (anything on the vine or a branch makes an arrangement look more expensive). At home, I put it all together with floating candles, and voilà! I had a festive holiday arrangement.

Candles in flowers always look beautiful, but for safety, you want to make sure they're absolutely secure in the arrangement. To do this, I tape floral picks onto glass cylinder vases so that these can be placed into the foam, anchoring them to the arrangement. This approach is perfect for candles but also works with just about anything that needs to be secured in foam. From teapots to highball votives to hurricanes, the possibilities are endless.

This recipe requires a cylinder vase. You can put a variety of candles in them, including pillar candles and large (3") or small (1") floating candles. These small cylinder vases are extremely versatile and good to have on hand for many kinds of arrangements.

INGREDIENTS

1 bunch of red or orange tulips

1 to 2 bunches of orange or yellow alstroemeria

1 bunch of sunflowers

1 bunch of berries such as ilex (red winter berries) or kumquats on the vine

1 bunch of lemon leaves or solidaster

2 blocks of floral foam

2 cylinder vases (2" to 3" wide, 6" to 8" high)

2 candles (pillar or floating)

Optional: pinecones, acorns, or anything with a stick that can be added in.

6 floral picks

Thick green floral tape

Wood rectangle container with plastic liner

1 Soak the foam and place it into the lined wood container. Both blocks should fit side by side.

2 Either cut or break the floral picks so that they're each about 5" long.

3 Tape one pick running vertically to the bottom inch of the vase, so that about 4" of the pick hangs down below the bottom of the vase. Secure the pick to the side of the vase using thick green floral tape. Tape 2 more picks to the vase, evenly spaced around the vase, so that the 3 picks align in a triangle shape. Wrap the tape around the picks and the vase a few times.

4 Repeat step 3 with the other vase.

5 Secure the vases in the wood container by inserting the picks into the foam until the bottoms of the vases are resting on the surface of the foam. Center each vase on either side of the container.

6 Place pillar candles directly inside the vases. For floating candles, fill the vases two-thirds full of water and place the floating candles inside.

7 Prep all the flowers.

8 Cut the tulip stems to about 5" to 6" long. Place half the tulips on each end of the container, angled out. You want the blooms to lie horizontal or facing downward, draped over the edges of the container.

9 Cut the alstroemeria stems to about 3" to 5" long. Place a couple stems on each side of the arrangement and throughout the middle, keeping them clustered. The flowers need to rise at least an inch above the top of the floral foam so that they hide the floral picks.

10 Cut the stems of the remaining flowers to about 4" long. Clustering each type of flower in groups of 2 to 3 stems, place them evenly throughout the arrangement.

11 Cut the lemon leaves or solidaster to about 4" to 5" long, then insert them sparsely but evenly throughout the arrangement, using them as accents.

CARE TIP: Since tulips grow after they're cut, be aware that if you're making this a day or two in advance, your tulips might look longer the next day. If so, recut and place them back in the floral foam.

DESIGN TIP: To create a vineyard feel, use a muted palette and insert small bunches of plum-colored champagne grapes (instead of kumquats) throughout.

89

floral foam

WINTER WONDERLAND

This is a strong, woodsy, winter arrangement, fitting for men or women who like bold, rustic designs. Bursting with textures and interesting shapes, it's a fun gift to give a few friends for the holidays since you can easily make several of these arrangements in one go. The easiest way to do multiple arrangements is to form an assembly line, completing the first step for each bowl, then the next step for each bowl, and so on.

You've probably noticed that in most designs, I usually start by arranging the flowers and then add in greens as accents. But for this arrangement, I start with the foliage and then add in the blooms. (If magnolia leaves aren't available, substitute lemon leaves, myrtle, or any shrubbery you like.)

PREP TIME: 15 minutes   **COOK TIME:** 30 minutes   **SEASON:** Winter   **DIFFICULTY:** 2   **COST:** $$$

the flower chef

INGREDIENTS

1 bunch of magnolia leaves

6 stems of antique green/blue or antique red/green hydrangea

1 bunch of Star of Bethlehem

1 bunch of purple or white lisianthus

1 bunch of fountain grass or wheat (depending on availability)

1 bunch of scabiosa pods

1 to 2 blocks of floral foam

3 brown or metallic soup bowls

CARE TIP: Leaf shine spray is made for arrangements like this that have a lot of foliage, and the spray makes the greenery really nice and shiny. You can also use it to clean any dusty spots off the leaves on potted orchids.

1 Soak the floral foam, then cut it in thirds and place each piece inside a bowl. Cut up small pieces of additional foam to fill in any gaps inside the bowls.

2 Using pruners, cut the magnolia branches into 6 pieces, so that each piece is about 3 times the height of each bowl. If you don't have pruners, you can bend the branches and snap them in half with your hands. If the stems are too thick to bend, then put the stem under your shoe while holding on to the top of the branch and snap it with your foot. I do this a lot with all kinds of branches!

3 Remove any leaves from the bottom third of the branches, approximately 3" to 4". In the first bowl, place one stem off-center and angled slightly to the left, inserted about 4" to 5" into the foam. Place another stem to the right of the first branch, angled out and to the right, inserted 4" to 5" into the foam. Repeat with the 2 other bowls.

4 Cut the remaining magnolia branches about 4" shorter than the tallest piece in each bowl. The goal is to create a leaf base in order to cover up most of the foam, while still keeping the asymmetrical shape. Place 3 to 4 of these shorter stems evenly throughout each bowl, inserting the stems about 3" to 4" deep.

5 Prep all the flowers. Cut the stems of half of the flowers to about 10" long and the other half to about 6" long.

6 Place 2 stems of hydrangea in each arrangement at the outer edges of the bowl, one on each side, with one stem slightly higher than the other. Position the taller hydrangea next to the tallest magnolia branch.

7 Insert the Star of Bethlehem evenly throughout each bowl.

8 Insert lisianthus evenly throughout each bowl.

9 Place a few stems of fountain grass angled outward near the hydrangeas in each bowl.

10 Add in scabiosa pods evenly throughout the arrangement, positioning them at various heights to make it look more organic.

DESIGN TIP: Instead of the separate smaller bowls, this would also look attractive as one larger centerpiece or on an entryway table. For that, I'd use a brown or metallic pedestal vase or serving bowl.

KNOCKOUT IN WHITE

Perhaps you're planning an elegant formal affair or a fancy wedding, and you want long, striking centerpieces. Or maybe you have a narrow credenza and you want a fabulous arrangement that will wow people. Instead of using long, rectangular vases—which can be really difficult to find—use multiple smaller vases set next to each other in a row. This creates the illusion of a single elongated vase and lets you tailor the arrangement to whatever size you wish.

In this all-white design, it's important to remember that when you're using only one color in an arrangement, texture is key. The best way to achieve texture is to use a variety of flowers with all kinds of shapes and petals. Mix round (roses, dahlias) with pointy (veronica, heather, stock), fluffy (hydrangeas, peonies) with stiff (thistle, Star of Bethlehem). Avoid flowers with large dark centers like gerbera daisies or anemones, which can be distracting if you want a pure white arrangement.

PREP TIME: 20 minutes   COOK TIME: 25 minutes   SEASON: Year round   DIFFICULTY: 2   COST: $$$$

INGREDIENTS

5 stems of extra-large white hydrangea

1 bunch of Star of Bethlehem

1 bunch of white garden roses (or 6 stems)

1 bunch of veronica

1 bunch of ruscus (or a few stems)

2 blocks of floral foam

3 to 5 small square mirror or silver vases

1 Soak the foam, then cut it into multiple chunks to fit into each of the vases. The foam can either be level to the top of the vases, or about ½" above. Just remember that the more foam that is exposed, the more flowers that are needed to cover it. Place the vases next to each other in a row to arrange as if they were one long, narrow vase.

2 Prep all the flowers.

3 Cut the hydrangea stems to about 5" long. Insert the stems in a row down the center of the vases, evenly spaced so that they cover the foam on all sides.

4 Cut the Star of Bethlehem to about 6" long and push them through the hydrangea blooms, distributing them evenly throughout the vases.

5 Cut the garden roses to about 6" to 7" long. Since they are expensive, add them in places that will make them the focus of the arrangement, like on the sides or toward the center. You can cluster 2 to 3 stems together for impact.

6 Cut the veronica to about 7" to 8" long. Add in 2 to 3 stems on either end of the arrangement so that the flowers extend about 4" to 5" beyond the length of the vases. Place a few more stems throughout the top of the arrangement, pushing the veronica through the hydrangea blooms and into the foam, so that the veronica rests on the blooms of the hydrangea.

7 Cut the ruscus to about 8" to 10" long. Insert 2 to 3 pieces in different areas on either end of the arrangement. Add a couple stems throughout the center to break up the white.

DESIGN TIP: To make a less expensive centerpiece that has a similar look, use bud vases, which hold only a few stems, and place numerous vases down a table. You'll use fewer flowers and still make a big impact.

loral foam

EVERYDAY JEWELS

This recipe is similar to Knockout in White (page 93), but we're making it a bit more casual by switching to jewel tones and a dressed-up wood container. The gorgeous purples and pinks are lusciously cozy, while the green hydrangea makes this centerpiece pop. This would be perfect for a backyard barbecue, laid-back wedding, or kitchen table centerpiece.

PREP TIME: 15 minutes   COOK TIME: 20 minutes   SEASON: Year round   DIFFICULTY: 2   COST: $$–$$$

INGREDIENTS

6 to 8 stems of mini green hydrangea

2 bunches of purple and/or fuchsia stock

Optional: 2 to 3 bunches of purple flowers (tulips, larkspur, lisianthus)

2 blocks of floral foam

Wood rectangle vase with plastic liner

1 Soak the foam, then cut it into chunks to fit into the vase. The foam can either be level to the top of the vase or about ½" above.

2 Prep all the flowers.

3 Cut the hydrangea stems to about 4" to 5" long. Insert the stems diagonally on both sides, facing outward and spaced evenly along the length of the vase.

4 Cut the stock to about 5" to 6" long. Add in a couple stems by each hydrangea, facing outward, starting at one end and working down to the other.

5 Fill any remaining open spaces with additional stock, making sure all of the foam is hidden from view.

6 If you're adding in other purple flowers, cut them to about 6" to 7" long. Place them next to, but angled away from, the stock.

DESIGN TIP: Before beginning the arrangement, use a hot glue gun to trim the box with ribbon. Keep it elegant with neutral colors, or do something funky with a patterned ribbon. For a personalized gift, you could have the recipient's initials engraved in the wood.

OH HAPPY DAY

Sunflowers are an instantly uplifting flower that can be dressed up or down and make a perfect gift for anyone—from expressing love to a close friend to giving thanks to an acquaintance. For an everyday cheerful arrangement, pair them with a yellow or green vase, and offset them with various shades of bright purple, green, and blue.

PREP TIME: 10 minutes   COOK TIME: 15 minutes   SEASON: Year round   DIFFICULTY: 1   COST: $$

INGREDIENTS

1 bunch of sunflowers

1 bunch of fuchsia or purple stock

1 bunch of green dianthus

1 bunch of thistle

1 block of floral foam

6" square yellow or green ceramic vase

CARE TIP: When transporting low arrangements, place them on the floor of the car. For tall arrangements, you can buckle them in the passenger's seat or backseat, or put them in an empty bucket on the car floor, surrounding the vase with newspaper to keep it from tipping over while the car is moving.

1 Soak the floral foam, then trim the foam to fit the vase and place it snugly inside.

2 Prep all the flowers.

3 Cut the sunflowers to about 5" to 6" long and place them evenly throughout the vase, inserting the stems an inch deep into the foam. The sunflowers should rise about 4" above the foam, since you want some height in the arrangement.

4 Cut the fuchsia stock to about 4" to 5" long. Add the stems in between and around the sunflowers.

5 Cut the dianthus to 3" to 4" long and place evenly throughout the arrangement. Cluster 2 to 3 stems of dianthus together if the flower heads are small to create a bigger impact.

6 Cut the thistle to about 6" long. Trim off any secondary stems and if they're long enough, use those too. Add in the thistle evenly throughout the arrangement. Push the thistle stems on the outer edge more deeply into the foam, so that they're resting on the edge of the vase.

the flower chef

FIVE-MINUTE FLOWERS

Whenever I have extra flowers from weddings and big events, I use the leftovers to make fun little designs for a side table or bathroom countertop. Really, this is the kind of arrangement you'd be most likely to find in my home—it's a quick and easy design that looks cute and uses flowers that would otherwise be tossed. This is like a last-minute weeknight dinner in which you root through your fridge, grabbing odds and ends, and whip up something that turns out to be surprisingly delicious.

I especially love using black flowers—such as black mini calla lilies, black dahlias, or 'Black Baccara' roses—to perk up almost any color combo. The dark blooms add dimension to bright colors, such as hot pink or a vibrant burnt orange, and they're also a nice accent to cool colors such as blue and green.

PREP TIME: 5 minutes   **COOK TIME:** 5 minutes   **SEASON:** Year round   **DIFFICULTY:** 1   **COST:** $–$$

INGREDIENTS

3 yellow or green roses

6 hot pink roses

3 to 4 black mini calla lilies or plum dahlias

Small piece of floral foam

3" to 4" square opaque glass or ceramic vase

DESIGN TIP: When using leftover flowers from a bouquet, try an inexpensive colored-glass vase from a thrift store or discount home store. Match one of the flowers to the color of the vase to tie it all together.

1 Soak the foam, then cut a piece to fit into the vase and place it snugly inside.

2 Prep the flowers and cut all the stems to about 4" long.

3 Place 3 hot pink roses in a triangle form in one corner of the vase.

4 Add the 3 yellow or green roses in each remaining corner.

5 Place the remaining 3 hot pink roses evenly spaced throughout, facing toward the outer edge.

6 Add in the calla lilies or dahlias wherever the foam is exposed.

TROPICAL DESERT

This design brings two very different landscapes—the desert and the tropics—together into one arrangement. It's all about experimenting, about making contrasts harmonize. The concrete planter is a nod to my urban neighborhood and how I occasionally come across miraculous vibrant flowers popping up out of cracks in the sidewalk.

The colors and textures here make this a gorgeous and intriguing gift, a more modern alternative to a potted orchid. If you're on a budget, this looks equally beautiful and simple using only the mokara orchids in the cement vase. This recipe also works well with leftovers from the Sunset Palette recipe (page 167). This recipe makes one big or two smaller arrangements, and it is long-lasting. Since this is a one-sided arrangement, it looks good set against a wall or mantel, or on an end table.

PREP TIME: 10 minutes   **COOK TIME:** 10 minutes   **SEASON:** Year round   **DIFFICULTY:** 1   **COST:** $$$–$$$$

INGREDIENTS

1 bunch of green or white 'Safari Sunset' (also called 'Safari Goldstrike')

3 stems of protea (mix of orange and yellow)

1 stem of green or yellow cymbidium orchid (or 3 to 4 blooms)

1 bunch of orange or yellow mokara orchids

Lime-green reindeer moss

1 block of floral foam

Small rectangle cement or gray terra-cotta vase

Optional: 3 to 4 water tubes (one for each cymbidium bloom)

1 Soak the foam and place it in the vase, slicing off the excess so that the foam is even with the top of the vase.

2 Prep all the flowers.

3 Cut half of the 'Safari Sunset' to about 5" to 6" long and place a few stems on opposite sides of the vase, resting on the edges.

4 Cut the proteas to about 5" to 6" long, and cluster them on one side of the vase.

5 Cut the cymbidium stem in half so that you have two pieces. Remove the bottom orchid blooms from each one. You now will have 2 cymbidium stems. Place the cymbidium stems toward the front of the vase, inserting them an inch into the foam.

6 Cut the mokara orchids to about 6" to 8" long. Remove the buds from the lower third of the stem. Place the stems toward the back of the arrangement. Angle the stems that are closer to the sides of the vase a bit outward for dimension.

7 Fill in any empty spaces with more 'Safari Sunset.'

8 Place 2 to 3 small pieces of reindeer moss in the front of the arrangement, in between flowers, to add color.

CARE TIP: If you're using cymbidium blooms left over from another arrangement, place a water tube filled with water on each bloom stem, since the stems on the bloom are too short to reach the water. Then place each water tube into the foam (see Autumn Light on page 143). You can buy water tubes at any floral supply or craft store.

BRANCH OUT

This extra-large statement piece makes a splash for an entryway and is perfect if you need a huge eye-catching arrangement for a bar at a wedding or special event. Although I do go light on the branches here, you can use this approach to create an over-the-top arrangement. To do so, use double the amount of branches and create a round symmetrical shape for a traditional design.

Since the last thing you want is for water to leak out of your arrangement, make sure to line the container if it's not waterproof. Or add a smaller plastic vase or bucket inside the container and fill that with the floral foam. If there's too much space between the two, fill the open space with newspaper to stabilize the smaller vase or bucket inside the main container.

PREP TIME: 15 minutes   COOK TIME: 35 minutes   SEASON: Winter/Spring   DIFFICULTY: 3   COST: $$

INGREDIENTS

1 bunch of blooming seasonal branches (quince, cherry blossoms, forsythia)

1 bunch of lemon leaves

2 to 3 blocks of floral foam (depending on size of planter)

Thick green floral tape

Gold spray paint

Plastic liner (a folded trash bag, cellophane, or specialty foil covered in plastic)

Urn or cement planter

DESIGN TIP: For a more upscale look, add in a base of hydrangea at the end.

1 Soak the foam. Working outdoors over a trash bag or newspaper, spray-paint about half the lemon leaves gold, covering both sides, and spray-paint the urn or container to match. Let the leaves dry for about 10 minutes, and let the urn or container dry completely.

2 Line the urn or container with plastic or insert a smaller bucket into it. Cut the foam to fill the inside. If you're using a bucket inside the container, place newspaper, bubble wrap, or some sort of filler around the sides to stabilize it.

3 Stretch multiple strips of floral tape across the top of the container, crisscrossing as you go so that the strips make a cross or a star shape over the top of the foam. Then wrap tape around the rim of the container to secure the strips you've just placed across the top.

4 Cut the thicker branches to about 3' long, using garden scissors on thinner stems and pruners for really thick stems, or place the end of the stem under your shoe and bend the branch upward to snap it. Place 2 to 3 of the straightest branches in the center of the vase, inserting the stems 6" deep in the foam so that they won't wobble.

5 Insert the branches into the foam according to how they naturally bend. For example, if the stem arcs to the left, place the stem on the left side of the vase so that it extends out and away from the vase. Create a loose circle of branches in the middle of the container by placing a cluster of 2 to 3 stems at 4 equal points around the circle. (Think of the vase as a clock and add the flowers at 3, 6, 9, and 12 o'clock.) Each cluster of branches should be fanning outward.

6 Cut the remaining branches a foot shorter than those you just placed, and add them, one at a time, around the outside of the circle you just formed. Make sure each branch is secure in the foam. You may have leftover branches, which is OK, since if you jam too many stems into the foam, the foam can crumble and break.

7 Take a step back and walk around the arrangement to get an overall view; it should look full and balanced.

8 Cut the lemon leaves to about 8" to 10" long and place them into the foam around the entire perimeter of the vase, creating a collar of foliage around the base of the branches. This is a good way to conceal any visible foam and tape.

SPANISH STEPS

With its trailing flowers and lush blooms, this arrangement was meant to capture the feeling of dreamy evenings dining al fresco under the stars in Europe, whiling away the hours with friends around candlelit tables in late summer. This design would look charming on a coffee table outdoors, or super-romantic set near a fireplace.

When it's in season, I like to use ornamental kale in my arrangements. Make sure the kale, which you can buy from florists or some delis and bodegas, has a long stem. Kale generally comes in green, purple, and white, and the touches of light pink and pops of yellow in the bouquet soften it up.

PREP TIME: **15 minutes**   COOK TIME: **20 minutes**   SEASON: **Year round**   DIFFICULTY: **2**   COST: **$$–$$$**

INGREDIENTS

1 bunch of peach or pale pink stock

2 to 3 stems of ornamental kale

1 bunch of plum ranunculus

1 bunch of red/purple hanging amaranthus

1 to 2 blocks of floral foam

6"-wide plant container, gray terra-cotta vase, or mauve ceramic vase

1 Soak the foam. Cut it in half and place one block inside the vase, cutting the other block into smaller pieces and placing them inside for a snug fit.

2 Prep all the flowers.

3 Cut the stock so that it is double the height of the vase. Remove the bottom third of the leaves. Place the stock evenly throughout the foam. This arrangement is meant to be slightly asymmetrical to add interest and texture. To get this effect, push some stems deeper into the foam on one side.

4 Cut the kale to about 7" to 8" long, removing any excess leaves on the stem. Insert the kale toward the outer edges of the arrangement, about 2" to 3" deep into the foam, spacing them out a bit.

5 Cut the ranunculus to about 6" long, and evenly distribute throughout the arrangement, clustering 2 to 3 stems together in each area. Push the blooms on the outer edges of the arrangement farther into the foam so they're shorter than the blooms at the middle of the arrangement.

6 Cut the amaranthus to about 6" long, placing them deep in the foam toward the middle of the arrangement so that the amaranthus stems are hidden and the amaranthus blooms drape over the rest of the arrangement and over and down the sides of the vase.

DESIGN TIP: If you don't have hanging amaranthus, substitute seeded eucalyptus, which has the same shape and a muted tone.

floral foam

GLITTERY JULEP CUP

Measuring around 4" to 6" high, silver or mercury julep cups are an easy way to add an elegant accent to any tabletop. Set near candles, they twinkle with reflected light—perfect for holidays or events. They look pretty when placed around a main centerpiece, and they're also lovely on their own or in little clusters on a cocktail table, a small desk, or as a thank-you gift. They are perfect additions to bedside tables if you're hosting out-of-town guests. The vase I used in this arrangement is just a bit larger than a julep cup, though it has the same look.

PREP TIME: 15 minutes   **COOK TIME:** 10 minutes   **SEASON:** Year round   **DIFFICULTY:** 2   **COST:** $$–$$$

INGREDIENTS

1 stem of white phalaenopsis orchid

1 stem of brown/red cymbidium orchid

3 stems of cream roses

1 bunch of lemon leaves

1 block of floral foam

Silver spray paint

4 to 5 water tubes (one for each phalaenopsis and cymbidium bloom)

Small silver fluted vase or large julep cup

1 Soak the foam, then cut it so that the top is even with the vase and it fits snugly inside.

2 Spray-paint the lemon leaves silver outdoors over a trash bag and let the leaves dry for about 10 minutes.

3 Fill 4 to 5 water tubes. Cut 2 blooms of phalaenopsis from the main stem at an angle. Place each stem in a water tube. Cut 2 to 3 blooms of cymbidium from the main stem at an angle, then place each stem in a tube.

4 Cut a few stems of lemon leaves to about 5" to 6" long and place them in the center of the vase, fanning out the leaves to cover most of the foam.

5 Prep the 3 rose stems and cut them to about 6" long. If they're closed, blow in the center of each bloom to help open them up. Place the roses close together, clustered in a triangle shape toward the front of the vase.

6 Place the cymbidiums where there's empty space, making sure to press the water tubes fully into the foam.

7 Put the phalaenopsis stems above the cymbidiums, pressing the water tubes fully into the foam so they're hidden. The phalaenopsis look better if the blooms overlap slightly. They can also hang just slightly over the side of the vase. Since these are very delicate flowers, they should be added last.

8 Cover any exposed foam with more silver lemon leaves. Gently turn some of the leaves, maneuvering them so that they nestle between the flowers in order to break up the colors.

DESIGN TIP: Use a riser to create a multi-level tablescape. Upside-down wood boxes or metalic vases, books, albums, and cake stands can all be used as impromptu risers.

the flower chef

5

THE GRID

If you place a bunch of tulips in a vase, the flowers will flop to one side because there's nothing to help hold them in place. That's where a grid comes in handy. Made out of crisscrossing strips of clear floral tape, the grid lets you position flowers exactly where you want them without them drooping over—which is especially necessary for more advanced arrangements, in which flowers need to be strategically placed. If you want a pristine, modern, tight arrangement, a grid is also the best way to go.

A snap to do once you learn how, making a grid is worth the extra few minutes in prep. Plus, it often saves time when arranging, because it lets you add flowers fairly quickly without having to worry about them leaning to one side or flopping over. A grid also is a great way to secure flowers if you're transporting them.

If you're making a lot of arrangements, you can always prep the vases a few days ahead of time. Some of the designs in this chapter can be made without a grid, but trust me, you'll find that it is much easier and faster to make them with this handy technique.

It doesn't matter if you add in the water before or after making the grid, but if you add it in before, use a paper towel to wipe around the sides and the rim of the vase so that it's completely dry. The tape will fall off if the vase is even a tad wet.

HOW TO MAKE A BASIC GRID

1 Wrap tape around the rim of the vase. This anchors the grid and also lets you remove the grid more easily for cleanup. [a]

2 Place parallel strips of ¼" clear floral tape, about 1" apart across the top of the vase. [b] Then turn the vase 90 degrees and add more strips of tape perpendicular to the others. [c] If you're using all thick-stemmed flowers such as hydrangeas and sunflowers, make the squares larger, or if you're using a lot of thin-stemmed flowers like freesia, ranunculus, and spray roses, make the squares smaller.

3 Wrap another layer of tape around the rim to secure the rows of tape across the top. [d]

4 There will be excess tape that will be visible down the sides of the vase. To remove it, take a knife and press firmly against the vase, right below the piece of tape around the rim of the vase. [e] Take the knife around the circumference of the vase, slicing the excess tape and peeling each piece off. [f]

5 Fill the vase three-quarters full with water.

CALM AND COLLECTED

I love anything jungle-like, and this arrangement, with its cool greens and sages, looks like you could stumble upon it while hiking in Costa Rica or Southern California. Light and fresh, these flowers always inspire a sense of calm. It's sort of like taking a deep, cleansing breath—this is the ideal stress-relieving flower arrangement.

A view of the water and stems through the glass is always lovely, but for a more sophisticated arrangement, you could line the vase in this design with ti leaves (see Timeless Elegance on page 133 as an example, and page 130 for the technique).

PREP TIME: **10 minutes**   COOK TIME: **15 minutes**   SEASON: **Winter/Spring**   DIFFICULTY: **2**   COST: **$$**

INGREDIENTS

3 stems of white hydrangea

2 stems of antique green or sage hydrangea

1 small bunch of viburnum

Palm fern leaves or any tropical leaves

Optional: ti leaves, white open roses

Clear floral tape

6" to 8" round vase

CARE TIP: Although this arrangement is sensitive to heat and direct sunlight, you can make it a day ahead of time if you spray the petals with water each day and keep it in an air-conditioned room.

1 Fill the vase three-quarters full with water. With the tape, make a 3 x 3 grid over the opening of the vase.

2 Prep all the flowers.

3 Cut the hydrangea stems to about 6" to 8" long, and the viburnum to about 7" to 9" long. If you're using roses, cut them to about the same height as the hydrangea.

4 Place one white hydrangea in any of the grid spaces, angling the stem so it points toward the center of the vase. Take the other two white hydrangeas and place them so they are evenly spaced apart from each other, with their stems also angled toward the center. This will make a round shape.

5 Add the green hydrangea in between the white.

6 Place the viburnum evenly throughout the arrangement, in between the hydrangeas.

7 Place a few stems of the tropical leaves evenly throughout the arrangement, in between the hydrangeas.

8 Rotate the arrangement a few times to make sure it looks balanced from different vantage points.

9 If using roses, add them to the outer edge of the arrangement, angling the blooms out, with the stems pointing toward the center. You don't want any stems sticking straight up.

WHAT GOES WHERE IN THE GRID?

It doesn't matter where on the grid you place the stems, as long as they're secure and spaced appropriately. Many—or no—flowers can go in each space of the grid; it just depends where you want blooms and how many can fit in each space. I usually add in thicker stems toward the center, since if the flower is too heavy, it can lean too far over the edge of the vase and fall out.

HERB JAR

Mason jars are readily available and are fun for holding country-inspired arrangements, or what I like to call "rustic modern" designs. This arrangement, which uses fresh herbs, is the perfect just-because gift for a foodie. It's also great for baby showers or outdoor barbecues.

Since this recipe will fill 3 smaller mason jars, you can divide the flowers evenly into 3 piles before arranging, or use all the flowers in one large jar. You can also mix and match the ingredients. This is a more expensive recipe, but feel free to substitute cheaper flowers of the same palette and shape.

PREP TIME: 10 minutes   COOK TIME: 25 minutes   SEASON: Fall/Winter/Spring   DIFFICULTY: 2   COST: $$$

INGREDIENTS

1 bunch of dusty miller

3 stems of pink peonies or pink garden roses

1 bunch of pink dahlias

5 to 7 stems of white or pink waxflower

1 bunch of white anemones or white ranunculus (depending on season)

Mixed bunch of fresh herbs: rosemary, thyme, sage

Clear floral tape

Large clear or blue mason jar or 3 smaller jars

Optional: burlap strips, lace, or twine

1 Fill the mason jar three-quarters full with water. With the tape, make a 2 x 2 grid over the opening of the jar.

2 Prep all the flowers.

3 Cut the ends off the dusty miller and place a few stems evenly throughout the grid, making sure that they're secure, since they have a tendency to droop.

4 Prep all the flowers, then cut the peonies (or roses) and dahlias to about 8" to 10" long, so the blooms are a couple inches above the rim of the jar. Place the stems evenly spaced throughout.

5 Cut the waxflower to about 8" to 10" long, then place the waxflower evenly throughout.

6 Cut the ranunculus or anemones to 8" to 10" long and add evenly throughout.

7 Pull up any stems that have slipped down into the jar. They should be able to breathe and open up.

8 Remove all foliage from the bottom half of the herbs. Insert the herbs evenly throughout the arrangement.

9 Tie twine, burlap, or lace in a knot around the rim of the vase to finish the look.

DESIGN TIP: As a chic alternative, create a spiraled bouquet instead of making a grid, and wrap it in decorative copper or gold aluminum wire to secure it. Cut the stems to about 6" long, then drop the bouquet into the mason jar.

BURST OF SUNSHINE

After a long day, this arrangement is so cheerful to come home to, with its vibrant mix of yellow, orange, and purple. It's like a bright burst of sunshine, bringing the happiness of nature indoors.

If, when making other arrangements, you accidentally cut the stems too short, this is a good way to use those flowers. You can mix and match various colors and types of flowers, and use a shorter vase to make a smaller version. I love this low rectangular vase because it has simple, clean lines, but it can be challenging to work with. If you're having trouble keeping the flowers from tipping over, it's best to work fast so that they can prop each other up.

PREP TIME: 20 minutes   COOK TIME: 30 minutes   SEASON: Spring/Summer   DIFFICULTY: 4   COST: $$$$

INGREDIENTS

1 bunch of blue thistle (or 5 to 6 stems)

1 bunch of white roses

1 bunch of orange tulips

1 bunch of sweet peas or hyacinths

1 bunch of purple or fuchsia stock

1 bunch of yellow or orange mini calla lilies (or 5 to 6 stems)

1 bunch of billy balls or yellow freesia

Low glass rectangle vase, 16" to 24"

Clear floral tape

1 Fill the vase halfway with water. Create a grid over the opening of the vase, placing about 12 pieces of tape an inch apart, across the width of the vase. Stretch one long piece down the center of the length of the vase. Wrap the tape around the rim of the vase to secure and trim the leftover tape on the sides of the vase. Since the vase is so long, this will be a bit time-consuming.

2 Prep the flowers and cut all the stems to about 4" long.

3 Distribute the flowers by type evenly throughout the grid. In the beginning, the flowers may flop around since there's so much space, but as you keep adding stems, they will hold each other up. You can place 2 to 3 stems in each square of the grid. Make sure the flowers are evenly distributed and balanced.

4 Add in the billy balls or freesia last, since they are very thin and prominent. The arrangement should have an even distribution of color, so adjust as needed.

DESIGN TIP: Add a layer of colored rocks or sand in the bottom of the vase, about ½" to 1" high, for an interesting visual effect. Make sure you do this first, before adding water to the vase.

FLAT TOP

Casual, creative, and nontraditional, horizontal arrangements are very popular right now and are frequently used as centerpieces. The trick to getting the flat-topped shape is to insert longer stems at a horizontal angle around the edges of the arrangement, and to put shorter stems pointing straight up and down in the middle of the arrangement. This design works especially well with flowers that have pointy tips or small buds. If ranunculus is out of season, freesia or spray roses are good substitutes.

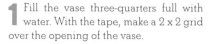

PREP TIME: 5 minutes   COOK TIME: 10 minutes   SEASON: Fall/Winter/Spring   DIFFICULTY: 3   COST: $

INGREDIENTS

1 bunch of orange, green, or red alstroemeria (with a yellow center)

1 bunch of yellow ranunculus

Clear floral tape

Small colored (orange, red, brown) square glass or pedestal vase

1 Fill the vase three-quarters full with water. With the tape, make a 2 x 2 grid over the opening of the vase.

2 Prep all the flowers.

3 Hold a stem of alstroemeria next to the vase. You want it to extend out of the vase about 3" on each side, so cut the stem accordingly. Measure and cut the rest of the alstroemeria against that stem.

4 Angle a few of the alstroemeria on each side of the vase so that the stems crisscross (which will hold them in place) and so that the flowers extend horizontally over the edge of the vase.

5 Cut the remaining stems of the alstroemeria an inch or two shorter, placing the majority of them in the middle of the arrangement, pointing straight up and down. Fill out the arrangement with the shortest stems. Rearrange the flowers until they look full and uniform.

6 Trim the ranunculus to about the same height as the tallest alstroemeria. Place small clusters of stems, angled out, throughout the arrangement. They can be slightly asymmetrical to give the arrangement movement.

7 Cut the remaining ranunculus 3" to 4" shorter and place them throughout the front and back near the center to fill out the arrangement.

DESIGN TIP: Look at how the stems are aligned in the bottom of the vase when you're working. Make sure they are spaced evenly apart and aren't clumped together.

SWEET AND SIMPLE

If you have a splashy vase you want to show off, or a vase with a pattern, you should keep the flowers simple to highlight the vase. This super-quick recipe is perfect when you're busy and have a nice decorative vase around. I like to make easy arrangements like this on days when I don't have a lot of energy and just want to plop flowers in a vase.

The key to this recipe is mixing round flowers (dahlias, mums, sunflowers) with pointy ones (tulips, snapdragons, Bells of Ireland), which provides contrast and makes a simple arrangement interesting.

PREP TIME: 5 minutes   COOK TIME: 5 minutes   SEASON: Winter/Spring   DIFFICULTY: 1   COST: $–$$

INGREDIENTS

1 bunch of pink roses or garden roses (or 5 to 6 stems)

1 bunch of peach hyacinths

Clear floral tape

Decorative vase

DESIGN TIP: Pick either the vase or the flowers as a focal point. In this design, it is the vase. Sometimes, flowers take a backseat.

1 Fill the vase three-quarters full with water. With the tape, make a 2 x 2 grid over the opening of the vase.

2 Prep all the flowers.

3 Cut the roses so that the blooms are a couple inches above the top of the vase. Place them on the left side of the vase.

4 Cut the hyacinths so that the flowers rest on the rim of the vase. Place them on the right side of the vase.

5 Rearrange the flowers a bit so that all the flowers are facing outward on their respective sides.

DESIGN TIP: I like to create my own decorative vases by wrapping them with fabric. It's easy to do—just cut a piece of fabric 2 to 3 inches longer than the circumference of the vase. Hot glue one end to the vase then wrap it tightly around the vase, fold over the other end to make a nice edge, and hot glue the finished edge to the vase. You can use material like burlap, linen, velvet, or lace, which gives the arrangement a rustic, sophisticated, or demure look depending on the occasion.

the flower chef

CONTRASTING CHIC

This is an arrangement I'd typically make for an office. It's artsy and elegant and the tuberose gives it a sublime, sweet fragrance. To make this arrangement funkier and more exotic, add in a bunch of dianthus.

PREP TIME: **20 minutes**   COOK TIME: **40 minutes**   SEASON: **Year round**   DIFFICULTY: **3**   COST: **$$$**

INGREDIENTS

1 bunch of tuberose

1 to 2 bunches of white lisianthus

1 bunch of white mini calla lilies

1 bunch of black mini calla lilies (or 5 stems)

1 bunch of Bells of Ireland (or 6 to 7 stems)

Multicolor pebbles or river rocks

Clear floral tape

Medium cylinder vase

1 Place the rocks at the bottom of the vase, about an inch high. Fill three-quarters full with water. With the tape, make a 3 x 3 grid over the opening of the vase.

2 Prep all the flowers.

3 Give the tuberose stems small cuts on a slant, keeping as much of the length as possible. Place the stems, angled outward, evenly throughout the vase, inserting 1 to 2 stems in each space on the grid.

4 Cut the lisianthus to about 10" to 12" long. Place a few stems in the front center of the vase, then add in a couple stems to each side. Set aside the rest for later.

5 Give the white calla lilies a small cut on a slant. Place them evenly throughout the arrangement, keeping the taller ones in the center and placing a few shorter ones (trim them if necessary) on the sides. They will prop up the lisianthus and other flowers. As the arrangement gets fuller, it will be easier to shape.

6 Give the black calla lilies a small cut. Place three stems on the left side, facing out. You want the innermost stem to be tallest and the outermost stems to be shortest. To do this, gently pull up the stems to the desired height after you insert them.

7 Take 2 more black callas and place them on the right side, facing out, adjusting the height as in the previous step. The black callas help give the design an asymmetrical shape.

8 Cut a few stems of Bells of Ireland to about the height of the tuberose. Add them in on the left side, spacing stems a few inches apart so that they have room to breathe. Cut less off the remaining stems of bells, so that they'll be the tallest flowers in the arrangement. Add those stems in throughout the center and on the right side of the vase.

9 Gently pull up any flowers that have fallen while arranging. If there are still empty spaces, fill out the arrangement with the remaining lisianthus, clustering the blooms together to create impact.

the grid

RAINBOW LOVE

This is one of my favorite arrangements because it uses so many types of seasonal flowers and lots of vibrant colors. And, just like a rainbow, each color is in its own distinct section. Most high-end florists stick with only 2 to 3 colors at a time, but I love a mix of bright hues. I think flowers are meant to be fun; someone once called my style "fruit salad" because of the amount of color variety I sometimes use. This design demonstrates one of my mottos: Don't be afraid to take risks or stray from convention.

As you're arranging this one, keep in mind that the exact placement of each flower isn't as important as keeping bunches of flowers together, making sure that each bunch is at a different height—but that all of the stems are still in water.

Prep time: 25 minutes   Cook time: 45 minutes   Season: Year round   Difficulty: 4   Cost: $$$–$$$$

INGREDIENTS

1 bunch of open orange or red oriental or Asiatic lilies

3 to 5 stems of mini green hydrangea

1 bunch of orange or red tulips

1 bunch of pink or purple ranunculus

1 bunch of billy balls

1 bunch of bear grass

Clear floral tape

Crushed blue glass/rocks/marbles

Medium cylinder vase

1 Place a layer of rocks, glass, or marbles inside the vase, about an inch or two high. Fill the vase three-quarters full with water. With the tape, make a 2 x 2 grid over the opening of the vase.

2 Prep all the flowers.

3 Cut all the lilies so that the blooms are about 6" to 8" above the top of the vase. Place them in the back right quadrant of the vase.

4 Place 2 hydrangea stems in the front right quadrant, so that the heads are a couple inches above the top of the vase. Place 1 to 2 stems in the front left quadrant and one in the back left, trimmed so that the heads are resting on the rim of the vase. The hydrangea in the back will help keep the rest of the flowers in place by taking up room in the arrangement.

5 Cut the tulip stems on a slant and place the entire bunch in the front left quadrant, behind the hydrangea. They should extend 3" to 4" out from the vase.

6 Cut the ranunculus to about 6" long and place them as a bunch in the front right quadrant, in front of the hydrangea.

7 Cut the billy balls to about 6" to 8" long. Divide the billy balls into 2 groups. Place a group on each side of the ranunculus, pulling one cluster of the billy balls up so it's a couple inches higher than the other.

8 Take the bunch of bear grass and cut off a few inches straight across the bottom, which will remove any dirt and make it easier to insert into the arrangement. Place the entire bunch into the back left quadrant of the arrangement between the lilies and the tulips.

9 Loop the top of added grass forward so it forms an arch, and then tuck the grass in between the flowers of the front left quadrant, behind the hydrangea. [a] The top of the grass will then stick straight out on the front right quadrant. If some of the shorter pieces of bear grass pop up, you can simply pull them out or tuck them back in between other blades of grass to stay put.

DESIGN TIP: Any time you bend a flower or greenery, whether it's bear grass, curly willow, or Bells of Ireland, be sure to do it last to finish off the look and get the exact placement you want.

PURPLE POWER

For this design, I wanted to create something that looks as if you walked through a field of flowers, gathered an armful, and took them home to make an arrangement that's both gorgeously organic and also quite elegant. The all-purple palette is soothing, and using just one color looks expensive, while the various types of flowers provide texture.

Since the eucalyptus hangs down over the vase, this is a good arrangement to try with any super-basic glass vase since it doesn't really matter what the vase looks like. When you're at the grocery store or farmers' market, pick out different types of flowers in the same color to replicate this design for any occasion, any time of year.

PREP TIME: 15 minutes   **COOK TIME:** 20 minutes   **SEASON:** Year round   **DIFFICULTY:** 2   **COST:** $$–$$$

INGREDIENTS

Half a bunch of seeded eucalyptus

1 bunch of purple lisianthus

1 bunch of purple larkspur or delphinium

1 bunch of purple anemones or scabiosa

1 bunch of open purple or blue irises

Clear floral tape

Medium glass vase

1 Fill the vase three-quarters full with water. With the tape, make a 2 x 2 grid over the opening of the vase.

2 Take the eucalyptus, trim an inch off, and remove the leaves from the bottom half of its stems. Place the stems evenly throughout the vase. Allow the stems to drape over the sides.

3 Prep all the flowers, leaving some greenery near the blooms. Leave the stems as long as possible, giving them a small cut on a slant.

4 Place most of the lisianthus and larkspur (or delphinium) throughout the middle of the arrangement. Cut the few remaining stems an inch or two shorter and place them near the outer perimeter of the arrangement, next to the eucalyptus.

5 Add in the majority of the anemones or scabiosa throughout the middle of the arrangement. Then cluster a few stems together and add them at the front of the vase. Gently pull the anemones or scabiosa stems out a bit so that the flowers point outward and have room to breathe.

6 Add in the irises evenly throughout, grouping 2 to 3 stems together for more impact.

7 Once the arrangement is full and even, gently grip your hand around all of the stems, right below the blooms, and pull the entire bouquet up a couple inches to allow the flowers to spread out and breathe. Carefully pull individual stems up toward you to fan the flowers out for a fuller look.

DESIGN TIP: To make the entire arrangement one color, you could also spray-paint the eucalyptus the same color as the flowers.

TOMATO CAN FLOWERS

Fun, funky, and bursting with colors and shapes, this lively arrangement is fitting if you're having an Italian dinner or if you simply want to create a festive tablescape. Although I use ranunculus in this as the featured flower, you could substitute small roses or solely use backyard flowers. If you don't have a tomato can, a coffee can works equally well.

PREP TIME: **10 minutes** COOK TIME: **15 minutes** SEASON: **Year round** DIFFICULTY: **2** COST: **$**

INGREDIENTS

2 handfuls of mixed flowers cut from the backyard (bougainvillea, asters, lantana, greenery) or 1 premade wildflower bouquet with a mix of flowers

1 bunch of orange ranunculus

3 to 4 very firm tomatoes on the vine

Clear floral tape

Empty tomato can

Optional: floral pick or kebab stick, thick green floral tape

1 Fill the can halfway with water. With the clear floral tape, make a 3 x 3 grid over the opening of the can.

2 Remove any leaves from the bottom half of the backyard (or bouquet) flowers and cut them to about 6" to 8" long. Place the mix of flowers evenly throughout the vase. Pull up any stems that fall down. The blooms should extend out from the vase an inch or two on each side.

3 Prep and cut the ranunculus to about 7" to 8" long. For the ranunculus that have multiple small buds on thinner, secondary stems, cut them off where they meet the base of the main stem and set aside.

4 Place the ranunculus evenly throughout the arrangement, clustering 2 to 3 stems together in some areas for impact. Pull the ranunculus up and out toward the edge of the arrangement so they are slightly higher than the backyard flowers. The design can be slightly asymmetrical.

5 If the tomatoes are small, about 2" in diameter, you can place their attached vine inside the can as described below. If it feels like the tomatoes are too heavy or the vine won't stay in the can, secure the vine to a floral pick or kebab stick with thick green floral tape. Cut the stick to the same height as the vase. Place the vine (whether on a stick or not), in the front left portion of the can, and rest the tomatoes on the can's rim or allow them to hang over the side.

DESIGN TIP: As an alternative, you could spray-paint the cans gold or copper for an inexpensive yet beautiful look. If you do so, I'd recommend sticking with white and cream flowers, adding in touches of buttery yellows and peaches or simple greens.

6

LINED
VASES

Elegant, polished, and very professional, vases lined with glossy green or black leaves are often used in upscale arrangements for homes, hotels, and restaurants. The leaves hide any messy-looking stems inside the vase, and the overall look is sleek and smooth—making it perfect for more modern arrangements.

Tropical ti leaves are the most commonly used leaves to line vases. But black ti leaves or zebra plant leaves, which are smaller and have thinner center veins, also work well. Most of the time, I use the bigger green ti leaves, since they are large enough to use in a variety of vase sizes and they're inexpensive (wholesale $4 to $7 for 10 stems). You can purchase ti leaves at a florist or flower mart. They're sometimes sold at farmers' markets and high-end grocers, and they can be special-ordered if you ask in advance.

Though it may seem like a good idea to hide floral foam inside a clear vase using ti leaves, I wouldn't recommend it. Floral foam can get crumbly and float around inside a clear vase, becoming trapped between the ti leaves and the glass, which isn't very attractive. This is why it's best to stick with opaque vases when you're using floral foam.

HOW TO LINE A VASE

Lining a vase can be very frustrating, but hang in there! After a few tries, it gets easier. You'll use two leaves for each vase for the following reasons: (1) If your vase is too wide and one leaf won't cover the circumference, the second one will, and (2) the second leaf holds the first leaf in place.

BASIC PREP

Ti leaves are very useful for lining vases, but you have to trim down the center vein before working with them. Doing this makes the leaf pliable, so that you can wrap the leaf and put it inside a vase. If you don't take out the vein, the leaf isn't as flexible and will snap. (You don't have to do this for smaller leaves, such as black ti and zebra, since those have thinner veins and are already flexible.)

To prep ti leaves, first cut the stem about an inch above where the stem meets the leaf (opposite the pointy end). Then, remove the center vein from the middle to the bottom end by placing the front of the leaf (shiny side down) on a table edge, lining up the vein against the edge and carefully shaving the center vein down with shortish strokes of a knife until

the leaf becomes pliable. Keep the knife almost parallel to the leaf, but ever so slightly pointed up. If you've ever shaved long strips of asparagus when you're cooking, this technique is similar. You can use a Swiss army knife, florist's knife, or even a small steak knife to remove the vein. Be patient because doing this correctly takes practice. I always joke that it's good that ti leaves come in bunches of 10, because I can still go through a few each time I line a vase!

METHOD 1: SHORTER VASES

This approach is for round or rectangular vases that are approximately 12" or shorter.

1 Prep two ti leaves, according to the basic prep instructions, to make them flexible.

2 Hold the bottom of a ti leaf in one hand and, using your other hand, wrap the leaf around your hand, shiny side facing out, so that the pointy end is showing. [a–b] If the vein is still too thick, making it difficult to wrap the leaf, remove more of the vein.

3 Put your hand with the leaf wrapped around it into the vase, letting the leaf unfurl just enough so that it's snug against the glass. Make sure that the tip of the leaf can be seen through the glass. [c–d] For a short vase (around 6" high), the ti leaf will be approximately the same height, so it will cover the entire inside of the vase.

4 Wrap the other ti leaf around your hand and let it unfurl inside the first ti leaf in the vase. This helps keep the first leaf in place. Or, to show the tips of the two leaves, place the bottom of the second leaf inside the center of the vase. [e] Then, following the first leaf, wrap the second leaf around the vase. [f]

5 Adjust the leaves to overlap so that there are no holes or gaps between them. [g]

6 Using scissors, trim down the leaves if they're poking above the top of the vase. [h] Don't worry about cutting smoothly; any jagged edges will be covered up by the flowers you'll be putting into the vase.

7 Fill the vase three-quarters full with water. This will also help keep the leaves in place.

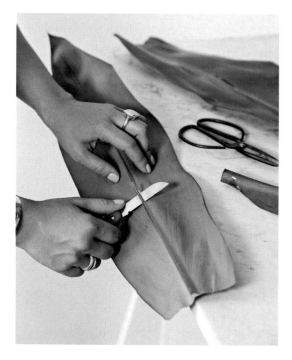

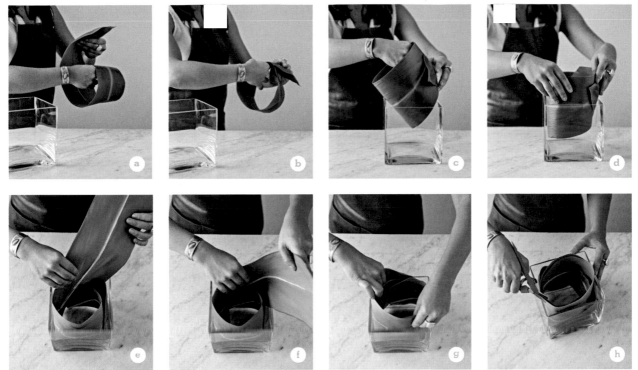

METHOD 2: TALL VASES

For a rectangular or cylindrical vase that is taller than 12", you can use Method 1. Simply continue to add more and more ti leaves, overlapping them in horizontal bands up the height of the vase until you reach the top.

Or, for a cleaner and more streamlined look, you can insert your ti leaves vertically into the vase instead of horizontally, using the following method.

1 Take one leaf, with the tip pointing down, and place it inside the vase so that its tip is at the bottom and the stem is sticking out of the vase. You don't need to remove the vein since the leaf is inserted vertically into the vase and therefore won't snap. The leaf will cover one or two sides of the vase, depending on how wide the vase is.

2 Continue inserting the leaves tip down so that they overlap and cover the interior of the vase completely.

3 Using the technique from Method 1, wrap a leaf around your hand. Place the leaf, which is now in a circle, horizontally inside the bottom of the vase. It will expand to fit the circumference of the vase, securing the vertical leaves against the glass. Repeat, inserting more ti leaves horizontally until the vertical leaves feel secure.

4 Trim the leaves so that they're even with the top of the vase.

5 Fill the vase three-quarters full with water.

FARMERS' MARKET FRESH

This perky, vivid arrangement was made on the fly—as some of the best arrangements are! I had picked up a bunch of sunflowers at a farmers' market, and once home, I was trying to decide what to make. Looking through my fridge, I spotted a few unused limes. I "lined" a small vase with them, and then cut the sunflowers short. It's a really cute and simple way to add a spark of color to any table or countertop.

This is a good example of how you can cut long-stemmed flowers short, then put them in low vases.

PREP TIME: 5 minutes   COOK TIME: 5 minutes   SEASON: Year round   DIFFICULTY: 1   COST: $

INGREDIENTS

3 stems of sunflowers

3 limes or 5 key limes

Small glass vase

1 Place the limes in the vase and fill the vase three-quarters full with water.

2 Prep and cut the sunflowers to a length so that the blooms will rest on the rim of the vase.

3 Place the sunflowers in the vase in a triangular shape, all facing out.

DESIGN TIP: For an impressive center-piece, you can fill a larger cylinder vase with any fruit and then top it with a topiary-style arrangement using the Five-Star Candelabra recipe technique (page 188).

TIMELESS ELEGANCE

In the same way that all-black outfits are always chic, all-white flower arrangements are a classic look that will never go out of style. To add even more elegance to this arrangement (and to make it seem really luxe), use a silver or mirrored vase. You could also use a cream or very pale yellow rose instead of white to soften up the arrangement.

PREP TIME: 20 minutes   **COOK TIME: 15 minutes**   **SEASON: Year round**   **DIFFICULTY: 2**   **COST: $$–$$$**

INGREDIENTS

5 stems of white hydrangea

1 bunch of white roses (or 8 to 10 stems)

1 bunch of white dahlias

2 ti leaves

Clear floral tape

5" to 6" square glass vase

1 Line the vase with 2 prepped ti leaves.

2 Fill the vase three-quarters full with water. With the tape, create a 2 x 2 grid over the opening of the vase.

3 Prep the flowers and cut all the stems to about 8" long. You can keep some leaves on the hydrangea at the very top, or remove them for an all-white look.

4 Place a hydrangea in each corner of the vase. If the blooms lean over too much, gently squeeze where the web of small stems meet, and make sure the entire stem is below the grid. This will tighten the hydrangea bloom. You can also turn the hydrangea bloom so it faces the other direction. If they're still too long, trim the stems.

5 Place the remaining hydrangeas in the middle to fill out the arrangement. The hydrangea blooms can overlap slightly, and they should be pressed against each other.

6 Add the roses and dahlias in small clusters evenly throughout the arrangement. Push some stems into and through the hydrangea blooms, so the roses and dahlias are resting on the hydrangea. Add shorter stems to the outer edges of the arrangement.

CARE TIP: To make an arrangement last an extra-long time (especially for weddings or events), buy a floral preservative spray at a craft or floral supply store. Mist all the flowers to create a high-sheen glossy look. The spray locks in moisture and helps prevent white flowers from browning.

EVERYDAY HYDRANGEAS

This is like a classic, basic pasta recipe, where you start with pasta (hydrangea) and toss in all your random veggies (a variety of other flowers) to come up with a delicious, easy meal. Simple and straightforward, it's a good starter recipe for even the most inexperienced flower chef.

While vases are most commonly lined with ti leaves, you can also line the inside of a vase with long flowers such as Bells of Ireland and branches such as curly willow. You can even cover the outside of a glass vase with paint or fabric. For this recipe, I add curly willow inside to complement the unisex palette of plum, white, and green.

PREP TIME: 15 minutes   **COOK TIME:** 20 minutes   **SEASON:** Year round   **DIFFICULTY:** 2   **COST:** $$$

INGREDIENTS

5 stems of white hydrangea

1 bunch of plum or red dahlias

1 bunch of light pink spray roses, ranunculus, or lisianthus

1 bunch of dark pink or plum spray roses

1 bunch of Bells of Ireland (or 4 to 5 stems)

Curly willow

Optional: lemon leaves or seeded eucalyptus

Clear floral tape

6" to 8" square or round glass vase

1 Wrap a few strands of curly willow around your hand and insert it into the vase, letting it expand to fit the interior of the vase.

2 Fill the vase three-quarters full with water. With the tape, create a 3 x 3 grid over the opening of the vase.

3 Prep and cut the hydrangea so that the blooms are slightly above the top of the vase.

4 Place one hydrangea in each corner, angled outward with the stems pointing toward the center. Place the last hydrangea in the middle of the vase. If any hydrangeas are leaning over the vase, reinsert them more toward the middle.

5 Prep and cut all the other flowers to about 8" to 10" long. Keep the flowers separated by type.

6 Place the dahlia stems through the hydrangea heads so that the dahlia blooms rest on top of the hydrangea. If the dahlias are sticking out, recut their stems so they fit snugly among the hydrangea heads.

7 Add the roses (or ranunculus or lisianthus) evenly throughout the arrangement, placing stems near the dahlias and clustering a few blooms together for impact. Rotate the arrangement midway through to make sure it looks balanced.

8 Add in the Bells of Ireland. To give the arrangement more shape and dimension, choose 2 stems of bells that are curving to the right and place them on the right side so that the blooms are slightly angled up and out. Choose 2 stems of bells that are curving to the left and place them on the left side so that the blooms are slightly angled down and out.

9 You can add one last stem of bells curving around the front of the arrangement. Place the stem in on the right side of the vase and curve it along the rim toward the left side of the vase. Tuck the top of the bells into the vase to secure it in place.

10 If using, add in the eucalyptus or lemon leaves to accent the flowers and break up the colors.

CARE TIP: If your curly willow branches seem dry or brittle and you're having trouble wrapping them, you can run hot water over them in the sink. That will soften them and make them more pliable.

CALLA BLUE

There's a lot you can do with ribbon. It's fun to mix and match colors, and ribbons let you play with hues not naturally found in flowers. Satin ribbons can also balance out harder-edged flowers and add extra texture to an arrangement. In this recipe, the navy ribbon punctuates the rich tones of the calla lilies while harmonizing with the soft shapes of the roses and oriental lilies. Sophisticated and bold, this is a unique Valentine's Day gift for someone who doesn't like traditional bouquets. It's also the perfect shape and size for a narrower space, if you want some flowers on your sideboard or bathroom vanity.

I like to use leftover flowers for this style of arrangement. The closed lily buds will open up within a couple days, making this delightful to watch as it fully blooms.

PREP TIME: 5 minutes   COOK TIME: 10 minutes   SEASON: Year round   DIFFICULTY: 2   COST: $$

INGREDIENTS

1 bunch of black mini calla lilies (or 5 to 6 stems)

3 to 5 stems of white, cream, or green roses

4 to 5 stems of closed oriental or Asiatic lilies

1' of blue ribbon

Clear floral tape

Small narrow rectangle vase (4" to 6" high)

1 Loop the ribbon around inside the vase. Fill the vase three-quarters full with water. Place 3 strips of tape evenly spaced across the width of the vase opening and 1 strip across the length of the vase opening, creating a 2 x 3 grid. Wrap another piece of tape around the top of the vase to secure the strips of tape.

2 Prep and cut all flowers so that the blooms are about an inch higher than the top of the vase.

3 Place the calla lilies together on the right side of the vase so that the blooms are all facing out.

4 Place the roses together on the left side of the vase so those blooms are also facing out.

5 Place 2 of the oriental lilies between the callas and roses and the other 2 to 3 lilies behind the roses, toward the back of the arrangement.

DESIGN TIP: If you don't have ribbon, you can use blue crushed glass, blue rocks, or blue marbles, all available at craft stores.

SUGAR MAGNOLIA

I really like the Grateful Dead's lyrics, melodies, and originality. This design was inspired by their song "Sugar Magnolia," which includes all sorts of references to plants, flowers, and nature. With its bright flourishes of hot pink and lime green, it's a sweet, happy arrangement that's as colorful and pretty as its namesake tune. Ideal as a thank-you gift or birthday present for a friend, it's a safe bet to give almost anyone.

PREP TIME: 20 minutes   COOK TIME: 40 minutes   SEASON: Year round   DIFFICULTY: 3   COST: $$$$

INGREDIENTS

4 to 5 stems of white hydrangea

1 bunch of green roses (or 10 to 12 stems)

1 bunch of hot pink roses (or 10 to 12 stems)

1 stem of pink cymbidium orchid

1 bunch of purple tulips

1 bunch of tropical leaves (zebra or ti)

Clear floral tape

Medium vase, any shape

1 Line the vase with the tropical leaves. Fill the vase three-quarters full with water.

2 With the tape, make a 2 x 2 grid over the opening of the vase.

3 Prep the flowers and cut all the stems to about 6" to 8" above the top of the vase.

4 Place the hydrangeas around the outer edges of the grid.

5 Insert the green roses into the front right quadrant, clustering them

together in a diamond or square shape. Push some of the roses into and through the hydrangea blooms, and place other roses right next to the hydrangeas.

6 Insert the pink roses, placing 2 to 3 together in the front right quadrant, 3 to 5 together in the back right quadrant, and 5 clustered together in the front left quadrant, inserting alternately through and next to the hydrangeas, just as you did with the green roses.

7 Cut the orchid stem in half, above a bloom, to make 2 orchid stems. If there are blooms near the bottom of either stem, pluck or cut them off.

8 Place the orchid stems in the arrangement, one in the front left quadrant in front of the pink roses and the other off-center in the middle of the arrangement, both pointing outward.

9 Place the tulips in groups of 3 evenly throughout the arrangement.

DESIGN TIP: If you trim any extra blooms off the cymbidium stems, don't immediately toss them. You can put the extra blooms in water tubes and add them to the arrangement, or put them in a bud vase.

FUNKY HEART

Sometimes you want to give someone a romantic, swoon-worthy gift, but classic red roses just aren't what you're looking for. Maybe your love is a little less traditional, or maybe you just want to make something cool, creative, and well, *funky*. If so, you wouldn't be alone. This arrangement became one of my signature designs—and was a top seller every Valentine's Day.

In floral design, prepping the vase and flowers is usually more time-consuming than the actual arranging. You can always get the vase ready a day or two ahead of time.

PREP TIME: 20 minutes   COOK TIME: 45 minutes   SEASON: Year round   DIFFICULTY: 4   COST: $$$

INGREDIENTS

1 bunch of horsetail

1 bunch of red roses (or 18 to 24 stems, depending on the rose head size)

1 bunch of bear grass

1 red anthurium (this is sold by the stem, not the bunch)

1 bunch of small red, black, or green ti leaves (or 2 stems)

1 block of floral foam

Glass rectangle vase

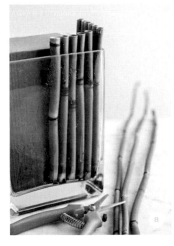

1 Soak the foam, then cut the foam into slices and chunks so that it covers the sides of the vase, leaving a ¼" gap between the foam and the vase. You want enough space for the horsetail to fit between the foam and glass, but not too much space, or else the horsetail won't stay in place. Getting the perfect fit can be time consuming and frustrating, so be patient.

2 Insert the horsetail stems along the sides of the vase, between the glass and foam, to create a solid wall of horsetail and conceal the foam. [a] Be careful not to nick the sides of the foam while inserting the horsetail or the foam will crumble. Trim the horsetail so it is level with the top of the vase.

3 Prep the roses and cut the stems to about 4" to 5" long. Starting in one corner, press several rose stems into the foam until their blooms rest on top of the vase. Add in more roses around these first blooms, to either side and toward the middle of the vase. You want to form a half-dome shape (like a wedge salad) centered around the back left corner of the vase, so it stretches diagonally from one corner to another and takes up half the vase.

4 Cut an inch off the bottom of the bear grass in a straight line. Using some force, push the ends of the bear grass into the foam in the back right corner, behind the roses. The grass will be standing straight up and down. Cut the top of the grass so it's about 12" in length. Bend the grass over so that it forms an arch and stick the other ends of the grass diagonally into the foam in the front left corner.

5 Take both ti leaves and cut the stems to a few inches. Stick the stems into the foam right behind the bear grass.

6 Bend each ti leaf backward, shiny side facing out, making sure not to crease them. Place them on the foam so that the leaves form a loop.

7 Cut the anthurium to about 4" long. Take the anthurium and insert it through the center of both ti leaves, into the foam, to hold them in place. Spread out the ti leaves so they're not overlapping.

DESIGN TIP: You can also attach horsetail to the outside by placing a rubber band or two around the vase, inserting the horsetail through them, then covering the rubber bands with black satin ribbon.

CITRUS SHINE

Bright, sunny, and cheerful, citrus is an easy way to add a special touch to a vase. And since it makes for such an upbeat arrangement, citrus-lined vases are wonderful for baby showers or bridal showers—they give arrangements a summertime feel, no matter the season.

Feel free to experiment with any type of citrus when lining a vase—limes, lemons, oranges, grapefruit—anything would work. It looks fancy, but there's an easy trick to this design: I place a slightly smaller vase inside a larger vase, filling the space in between with the sliced fruit. The key is to make sure that the smaller vase is only about ¼" to ½" narrower than the larger vase, since the narrower the space, the less fruit you need to fill it.

PREP TIME: 15 minutes **COOK TIME: 20 minutes** **SEASON: Year round** **DIFFICULTY: 2** **COST: $$$**

INGREDIENTS

1 bunch of orange tulips or yellow/orange parrot tulips

1 bunch of yellow tulips

1 bunch of orange spray roses or 8 to 10 stems of regular roses

6 lemons

3 stems of lemon leaves

Thick green floral tape or rubber bands

Smaller vase, pint glass, or plastic storage container

Medium cylinder vase

1 Fill the smaller vase, pint glass, or plastic container three-quarters full with water. Place it inside the medium vase.

2 Slice the lemons about ⅛" to ¼" thick depending on how much space there is between the two vases.

3 Place the lemon slices in between the two vases, until the space is entirely lined with lemon slices. The slices will overlap. You can cut the lemon slices in half to better fit at the top of the vase.

4 Prep all the flowers.

5 Spiral the tulips together so that the orange and yellow flowers are evenly mixed. Secure the bouquet with floral tape or a rubber band and set aside.

6 Spiral the roses together. Secure with floral tape or a rubber band.

7 Cut the stems of each bouquet so that the flowers rest on the edge of the vase.

8 Place the bouquets side by side inside the inner vase. If the arrangement doesn't look full or round enough, fluff or tug gently at the flower heads to create a fuller, more domed look.

9 Cut the lemon leaves to 3" to 4" long. Create a collar of leaves around the flowers by placing the stems inside the inner vase, so that the leaves drape over the entire circumference of the outer vase.

DESIGN TIP: You can really use anything to line the vase—berries, seeds, legumes, or candy, which is especially colorful for the holidays—although be mindful of the temperature, to make sure the candy doesn't melt. It's also fun to match the flowers to what you're using to line the vase. So if you use orange slices, use some orange flowers. If you use limes, use a bright green flower like a spider mum or button mum to tie it all together.

the flower chef

AUTUMN LIGHT

Bring a little sunshine into a dark autumn day with this arrangement. The rich colors make this design strong and vibrant, while the splashes of yellow cheer up any room. This would be perfect to make for poker night, or to give as a gift for a friend.

In this arrangement, since the orchid stems are too short to reach the water in the vase, you'll need to insert the blooms into water tubes.

PREP TIME: 15 minutes **COOK TIME:** 10 minutes **SEASON:** Fall/Winter/Spring **DIFFICULTY:** 2 **COST:** $$–$$$

INGREDIENTS

2 bunches of plum, red, or black ball dahlias

1 stem of yellow or green cymbidium orchid

2 small black/dark ti leaves

Clear floral tape

6 to 7 water tubes (depending on number of orchid blooms used)

4" to 5" square glass vase

1 Line the vase with the ti leaves. Smaller ti leaves bend easily, so you don't have to remove the vein.

2 Fill the vase three-quarters full with water. With the tape, make a 2 x 2 grid over the opening of the vase.

3 Prep and cut the dahlias to about 6" long. Trim off any secondary bud stems from the main dahlia stem and set aside.

4 Insert the dahlias evenly throughout the grid. The flowers can slightly overlap, or you can pull them up and out a little to give them a taller, cubic shape.

5 Cut the flowers off the main cymbidium stem, trimming the blooms as close to the main stem as possible to get the longest possible little stem.

6 Prepare the water tubes by slitting the openings to enlarge them for the orchid stems. Fill the water tubes with water, and insert each cymbidium bloom into a tube.

7 Place the orchids in the water tubes throughout the arrangement. Make sure the water tubes are hidden inside the arrangement so that you only see the flower. You can cluster 2 to 3 orchids together for visual impact.

DESIGN TIP: If you have a cymbidium orchid plant in a pot, you could use it for this arrangement instead of a cymbidium stem. Just snip the blooms off the plant, and use the same way as instructed above.

ORGANICALLY OVERLAPPED

The combination of bear grass and sunflowers all tumbled on top of each other makes this arrangement look natural and textured. This is a layered arrangement, where you add overlapping groups of flowers at different heights, sort of like stadium seating.

You'll need a lot of flowers to achieve this look, so it's best to use round-shaped larger blooms that will cover more surface area. Some of my favorite flowers to overlap are sunflowers, gerbera daisies, dahlias, and anthurium blooms (which look very exotic).

PREP TIME: 10 minutes   COOK TIME: 25 minutes   SEASON: Summer/Fall   DIFFICULTY: 3   COST: $$–$$$

INGREDIENTS

5 to 6 bunches of one type of flower, such as sunflowers

1 bunch of bear grass

Narrow rectangle vase

1 Cut an inch or two off the bottom of the grass. Wrap the entire bunch of grass around your hand, as you would do with a ti leaf, and place the grass inside the vase. Fill the vase halfway with water.

2 Prep and cut one bunch of flowers so that the blooms rest on the rim of the vase. Place the flowers evenly throughout the vase, facing outward. These flowers will provide support for the taller flowers, and all the flowers will overlap somewhat. It's a bit of a balancing act!

3 Prep and cut another bunch of flowers so that the blooms are 6" above the top of the vase. Place them evenly throughout the vase, facing outward and resting a bit on the shorter flowers.

4 Prep the third bunch of flowers, but leave them long, so that they'll be the tallest stems in the arrangement. Place them in the center of the vase, and slightly turn the flower heads upward (being careful not to pop or snap the flowers off). You can add in 1 or 2 rows of flowers in the center, depending on how much room you have.

5 Cut the stems of the remaining bunches of flowers to fill in any empty spaces and to make it all look symmetrical.

DESIGN TIP: Be sure the stems are going inside of whatever you're using to line the vase. It's common to place a stem inside the vase only to have it poke out and be visible between the liner and the vase (whether the liner is a ti leaf, curly willow, or bear grass).

CLASSIC CALLAS

There's something so simple and stylish about white calla lilies. Long, lean, and elegant, they shine on their own, in a simple glass or silver vase. This arrangement can easily spruce up any space, from your kitchen table to a black-tie wedding.

To increase the curves of the calla lilies, keep them out of water for an hour or so, then gently bend the stems in their natural direction. The size of your vase and your budget will determine how many calla lilies you buy, which will in turn make the arrangement look either minimalist or full. Either way, it will be beautiful.

PREP TIME: 10 minutes   COOK TIME: 20 minutes   SEASON: Year round   DIFFICULTY: 2   COST: $$

INGREDIENTS

2 bunches of large white calla lilies

1 bunch of Bells of Ireland

1 ti leaf

Clear floral tape

Tall cylinder glass vase

1 Line the bottom of the vase with the ti leaf. You only need one ti leaf, since you're just lining the bottom of the vase and the narrowness of the vase will keep it in place.

2 Fill the vase three-quarters full with water. With the tape, make a 2 x 2 grid over the opening of the vase.

3 Give the calla lilies a small cut on a slant. Divide the callas into groups depending on which way their stems bend.

4 Place the callas evenly throughout, based on how the stems naturally bend. Straightest stems should be in the middle of the arrangement, and stems bending right should be on the right side of the vase; left-bending stems on the left. Make sure that when you place them in, the callas are bending outward and not facing inward.

5 Prep the Bells of Ireland and cut them so that they're the same height as the callas, or slightly taller. Place the stems of bells evenly throughout, recutting them on the outer edges so they're an inch or two shorter than the others. You may not need to use all of the stems of callas or bells—it should just look even and balanced.

DESIGN TIP: If you want extra height for the calla lilies, you can soak a piece of foam and cut a piece to fit the vase. Then wrap the ti leaf around the foam and place in the bottom of the vase.

lined vases

7

FREEHAND ARRANGEMENTS

Freehand arrangements are done without the help of floral foam or a taped grid to plan flower placement. When I was starting out as a floral designer, this is the only kind of arrangement I made—because it was all that I knew how to do! It wasn't until a couple years after I started my business that I began using taped grids and all the other tools that made my life a lot easier. Although these arrangements might seem simple (you just toss a bunch of flowers into a vase, right?), in reality, these types of designs can be the most challenging to master since you don't have any placement tools to help you along. So don't worry if it takes you a while to get the hang of these.

Be creative. Freehand designs are meant to be made on the fly using materials you already have. Think of interesting ways to use your flowers. Twist them around, submerge them in water—experiment and don't be afraid to be equally adventurous with your choice of vase. But as with any arrangement, highlight either an interesting vase or an interesting flower combination, not both at once. And most important, the vase and flowers should complement each other, not clash.

It can be tempting to keep adding elements to your freehand design, but remember to occasionally stop, step away, and reassess. Sometimes less is definitely more!

DOTTIE'S TULIPS

My grandmother and I were very close, and she was always a source of encouragement to me. Toward the end of her life, I had just started my floral business, and she was one of the first people I told about my idea for this book. After she passed away, I created this arrangement of tulips, her favorite flower, to commemorate and celebrate her life along with my grandfather Joe's.

This design is my interpretation of a stacking technique, where you stack flowers in layers on top of each other, instead of spiraling, in order to get a balanced mix. After stacking, you gather stems into a bouquet. I had struggled several times to get this technique to work, and only by tweaking the method in various ways did I finally get the look I wanted. Which is why I always say that in design, there's really no right or wrong way—only what works. Feel free to play with different color combinations, or use this technique for other thin stems like mini calla lilies, irises, or ranunculus.

PREP TIME: 10 minutes **COOK TIME:** 15 minutes **SEASON:** Year round **DIFFICULTY:** 2 **COST:** $$

INGREDIENTS

1 bunch of yellow tulips

1 bunch of peach tulips

1 bunch of solidaster

Beige rocks or crushed shells

Clear elastic ponytail holders

Narrow glass rectangle vase

1 Run water over the rocks or shells to remove any debris, and place them in the bottom of the vase, about an inch high. Fill the vase three-quarters full with water.

2 Prep the tulips, then divide the 2 bunches of tulips evenly into 3 separate piles, so that each pile has an equal mix of peach and yellow tulips.

3 Spiral a mini bouquet for each of the 3 piles of tulips. Secure each bouquet with a ponytail holder, about halfway up the stems. Cut the stems to about 6" long.

4 Place the first bunch of tulips vertically against the right side of the vase. Stack the other 2 bunches next to each other so they're slanted diagonally into the vase, blooms angled to the left. You may have to cut the second and third bunch a bit shorter in order for the arrangement to be slightly slanted. Trim ½" at a time so that you don't end up cutting the stems too short.

5 After the third bunch of tulips is in place, fill the empty space on the left side with the solidaster and place a few stems of solidaster in between the tulips.

CARE TIP: Wrap drooping tulips in brown paper or newspaper, then place them in the fridge for a few hours so they perk back up. The cold will also cause the petals to close up again.

BEACHY BLOOMS

This is a variation on Dottie's Tulips, using the same color palette but making a taller arrangement and incorporating sand. I love using sand—it softens flowers and helps anchor the tulips. It's a more relaxed look, and a stunning statement piece for an entryway or buffet.

INGREDIENTS

1 bunch of yellow tulips

2 to 3 stems of peach gladioli

1 bunch of Star of Bethlehem

Clear floral tape

1 bag of white decorative sand (28 ounces)

Medium rectangle vase

1 Add 2" to 3" of sand to the vase, then slowly add in water until the vase is three-quarters full. The sand will make the water cloudy, but it should settle after a few minutes.

2 Cut the tulips to 5" to 6" long so the top of the blooms will be a few inches below the top of the vase when submerged. Secure the tulips together at the bottom of the stems using the clear floral tape. Submerge the tulips under the water, inserting the stems deep into the sand on the left side of the vase.

3 Cut the gladioli so that they're about 8" to 10" above the top of the vase. Insert the stems into the sand so they stand straight up against the right side of the vase.

4 Spiral the Star of Bethlehem flowers together and secure them with clear floral tape. Cut the stems to about 6" to 7" long. Place the bouquet at an angle behind the gladioli, so that the blooms are resting on the left side of the vase, extending a few inches out, and the stems are angled to the right.

THE PROVENÇAL

This arrangement was inspired by the colors and culture of Provence. With its vivid yellows, blues, and greens, this design is meant to evoke the warmth and sun in that part of France. Just like Provence, this arrangement also has a lot of life to it—and it would be ideal for a party or baby shower. I made this arrangement for the first event I ever did, a Bastille Day party, and I almost had a panic attack pulling all the flowers together. But despite my stress, the party was a smashing success—and the flowers looked professional.

As with most freehand arrangements, this design balances the stems and flowers against each other to form the structure. Getting this right requires some finesse, patience, and practice.

PREP TIME: **15 minutes** COOK TIME: **25 minutes** SEASON: **Year round** DIFFICULTY: **3** COST: **$$–$$$**

INGREDIENTS

1 extra-large blue hydrangea

1 bunch of blue delphinium (or 4 to 5 stems)

1 bunch of yellow lilies (or 3 to 4 stems)

1 bunch of Bells of Ireland (or 2 to 3 stems)

2 to 3 stems of curly willow

Narrow oval vase

1 Wrap the curly willow around your hand and place it deep inside the vase. Fill the vase halfway with water.

2 Prep all the flowers.

3 Cut the hydrangea to about 8" long and place the stem on the right side, allowing the blooms to hang slightly over the edge of the vase.

4 Cut the delphinium so they're about 10" to 12" long. Place the delphinium into the vase to the left of the hydrangea, so that the flowers are angled out and to the left.

5 Cut the lilies to about 6" to 8" long. Place a few stems on the left side of the vase, in front of the delphinium, so that the flowers are angled out and to the left. Then place a few more stems on the right side of the vase, inserting them into and through the hydrangea blooms.

6 Cut the Bells of Ireland to about 10" to 12" long and place them to the far left of the vase so that they stick out. They should point up and out to the left.

7 Place a few strands of curly willow in the vase by the bells, trimming the top of the willow to the same height as the bells.

PRETTY IN PASTIS

This is a variation on the Provençal using a similar color palette, with different flowers and a different vase. It's shorter and uses a bubble bowl (a round vase shaped like its name), which makes it a less expensive arrangement.

INGREDIENTS

1 to 2 stems of blue hydrangea

1 bunch of irises

1 bunch of white ranunculus

5 stems of yellow tulips

Bubble bowl

1 Fill the bowl three-quarters full with water.

2 Prep the flowers and cut all the stems to about 6" to 7" long.

3 Place the hydrangea in the back left of the bowl so that the head is resting on the rim of the bowl. It's OK if it hangs down a bit.

4 Place the irises together on the right side of the bowl, toward the back, so that they are taking up about a third of the bowl and are angled out. The front stems, closest to the top of the bowl, can be cut shorter.

5 Place the ranunculus together as a single cluster in the front center of the bowl.

6 Place 3 stems of tulips to the left of the ranunculus and 2 stems on the other side of the tulips to break up the color.

DESIGN TIP: In the Provençal arrangement, you can also substitute irises for the lilies, and campanula for the delphinium.

SHABBY CHIC

Although I love bright, vibrant colors for celebrations, I'm drawn to soothing color palettes for everyday arrangements. Some of my favorite colors are blue and sage, so when dusty miller became trendy, I was on board. This is a relaxed arrangement that is a bit rustic yet feels very romantic—perfect as a gift or on a side table. Another major plus: It's super-simple to make.

PREP TIME: 5 minutes   **COOK TIME: 10 minutes**   **SEASON: Year round**   **DIFFICULTY: 1**   **COST: $–$$**

INGREDIENTS

6 to 8 stems of dusty miller

1 bunch of white or cream open roses (or 5 to 6 stems)

2 to 3 stems of dried lotus pods (or any dried pod)

Square wood box with plastic liner

Optional: 1 block of floral foam

1 Fill the box liner three-quarters full with water. You can also use floral foam if you would rather not work freehand.

2 Cut the dusty miller to about 4" to 6" long. You want to create a loose base of dusty miller that is fairly flat and rests on the rim of the vase.

3 Prep the roses, making sure the blooms are very open. If they're closed, push the outer petals out gently. Don't mess with them too much or you'll have brown petals the next day. Cut the roses just tall enough so that the blooms can rest on the dusty miller, and place the roses in the vase. They should either be all bunched together or you can place 3 in one corner and 2 diagonally across in the other corner.

4 Place a single lotus pod in the middle of the arrangement, and another in a front corner, nestled next to the roses.

DESIGN TIP: As a variation on this arrangement, you could also make this into a bouquet. Start out holding the dusty miller in your hand, then pull through the roses and lotus pods with your other hand.

VINTAGE MODERN

This design is a fusion of shabby-chic flowers (curly willow and hydrangea) with clean and classic calla lilies, all arranged in a structured, artistic way. It's a sophisticated arrangement and would make an ideal gift for a person with impeccable style. It also looks beautiful set against a fireplace, in a foyer, or on a dresser.

In this arrangement, the flowers are clustered together by type, a technique that is called "blocking." You can block flowers in any arrangement to create a stark, modern look.

PREP TIME: **15 minutes** COOK TIME: **25 minutes** SEASON: **Year round** DIFFICULTY: **3** COST: **$$$**

INGREDIENTS

1 bunch of white oriental lilies

1 bunch of large white calla lilies

5 stems of blue hydrangea

1 bunch of green hanging amaranthus

1 bunch of curly willow

Medium rectangle vase

1 Wrap a few stems of curly willow around your hand and insert it into the vase. Fill the vase three-quarters full with water.

2 Prep the flowers, then give all the stems a small cut on a slant. You want the stems to be as long as possible.

3 Place the entire bunch of oriental lilies in the right back of the vase.

4 Insert the calla lilies stretching diagonally across the entire front of the vase, so that the blooms are in the front left corner, facing out, and the stems end in the front right corner.

5 Insert the hydrangeas. Place 2 in the back left and another in the front left. Then place 2 in the front right so they hang over the rim of the vase a little. It should all look lush and full.

6 Place the entire bunch of amaranthus in the front right corner, so that the stems point straight down and the blooms drape over the vase. You can keep them extra long so they drape onto the table, or cut them to end right above the bottom of the vase.

7 Place a few branches of curly willow as accents throughout the arrangement. The branches should point outward. Trim the tops of the curly willow so they're a few inches higher than the lilies.

ALLE'S ROSES

Alle, whose company was one of my very first clients, was constantly receiving flowers from her then-boyfriend and now-husband, Don (a keeper, right?). An extraordinary businesswoman, Alle has a nontraditional, modern style and loves unexpected arrangements. One Valentine's Day, I created this arrangement for Don to give Alle. Unlike the usual lush, red rose bouquet, this design is streamlined while still being completely romantic. Perfect for Alle—or for anyone who wants an artful romantic surprise.

In this recipe, I use a pretty satin ribbon to tie the stems. I used to buy whatever cheap ribbon was on clearance, but I've since realized that it's worth the extra few bucks to use higher-quality ribbon. I prefer to use a satin ribbon with wire inside so that it bends easily and stays put.

PREP TIME: 10 minutes   COOK TIME: 15 minutes   SEASON: Winter/Spring   DIFFICULTY: 2   COST: $$

INGREDIENTS

1 bunch of red roses (or 12 medium/long-stemmed roses)

1 bunch of pussy willow

12" to 15" of purple or black satin ribbon

3 corsage pins (cut short with floral clippers or a wire cutter, so that each pin is ½" long)

Thick green floral tape

Medium rectangle vase (ideally 12" to 16" high)

Black pebbles or river rocks

DESIGN TIP: When using ribbon, fold 1" to 2" of the end of the ribbon over and tuck it underneath itself to create a nice edge before securing it.

1 Add a layer of rocks inside the vase, 1" to 2" high, rinsing them off first. Fill the vase halfway with water.

2 Cut the ribbon into 3 pieces, each about 4" to 5" long. Cut 3 pieces of thick green floral tape, each about 4" to 5" long, and place on the edge of the table to grab easily.

3 Prep the roses and divide them into 3 groups of 4 stems each.

4 Take a group of roses and leave the stems on as long as possible, giving them only a small snip at the bottom. Take a few stems of the willow and place in between the roses, so that the willow is 8" to 10" above the roses. Cut the bottom of the willow the same length as the roses.

5 Secure the bunch toward the middle with a piece of floral tape.

6 Wrap the ribbon around the bunch. Fold over the end of the ribbon so that it creates a finished edge. Secure with a corsage pin. Place the bunch in the back left corner.

7 Repeat steps 4 to 6 with the next group of roses, except cut the stems about 3" to 4" shorter than the first group, and place in the back right corner at an angle.

8 Repeat steps 4 to 6 with the last group of roses, cutting the stems so that the rose blooms are right above the top of the vase, and place in the left front corner at an angle.

DESIGN TIP: If giving this as a gift, take a long piece of ribbon and tie it around the vase, letting the tails hang down.

DAY OR NIGHT

Understated and elegant, this arrangement is like a perfect pair of dark jeans—it can easily be dressed up or down. Pale green roses in a gold vase would make it fancy for a holiday or dinner party; pink roses in a galvanized tin container would make it laid-back for a luncheon. If you want to jazz this up, add in a thin-stemmed flower of any color—such as freesia or ranunculus—to the hydrangea bouquet or spiraled in with the roses.

You can also make this design on a larger scale for bigger impact. Simply secure 3 to 4 bouquets of flowers with floral tape or a ponytail holder, then drop the bouquets into a vase. I call this the "side-by-side" technique, and it's better to use this technique with opaque vases so that you don't see the tape, if that's what you choose to use.

PREP TIME: 10 minutes   COOK TIME: 10 minutes   SEASON: Year round   DIFFICULTY: 2   COST: $$

INGREDIENTS

3 stems of white hydrangea

1 bunch of green, purple, peach, or pink roses (or 6 to 8 roses, depending on vase size)

Optional: 1 bunch of freesia or any thin-stemmed flower

Thick green floral tape or clear elastic ponytail holders

Small gold vase

1 Fill the vase three-quarters full with water. If you're using freesia or any other thin-stemmed flower as an accent, decide if you want to spiral it in with the roses or pull it through with the hydrangea.

2 Prep all the flowers.

3 Spiral the roses and secure the bouquet with thick green floral tape or a ponytail holder just below the bottom of the blooms.

4 Spiral the hydrangea together and secure the bouquet with thick green floral tape or a ponytail holder just below the bottom of the blooms.

5 Measure the two bouquets against the vase so that the blooms rest on the rim of the vase. Cut both bouquets to the same height.

6 Place the two bouquets next to each other in the vase, facing out. The stems of the bouquets should crisscross inside the vase.

DESIGN TIP: If you're making this arrangement in a glass vase (either a small cylinder or bubble bowl), wrap ribbon around the tape on each bouquet to conceal it and secure with a corsage pin cut short. You can also go for a kitschy look by adding fun elements like feathers to one of the bouquets.

the flower chef

FASCINATOR FLOWERS

I love the hats that British women wear at weddings. Elaborately sculpted and dotted with fabulous feathers, flowers, and bows, the hats look so precise and regal—and so carefully perched on their owners' heads. This arrangement was inspired by those wonderful hats and is likewise ideally suited for a fancy bash, like a wedding, bar mitzvah, or anniversary party. The flowers here are placed just so in the vase, floating within the glass, and the willow gives the arrangement its dramatic flair and towering height. The delphinium is also a nod to gorgeous, well-manicured English gardens.

To achieve this floating effect, I use a "suspending" technique where I balance the stems inside the vase by angling and crisscrossing them against the sides of the vase. It's clean and simple and elegant looking. This is also a good example of how to make an arrangement wider and taller by carefully propping and balancing flowers against the vase.

PREP TIME: 15 minutes   COOK TIME: 45 minutes   SEASON: Year round   DIFFICULTY: 4   COST: $$$

INGREDIENTS

1 bunch of blue or white delphinium

1 bunch of white dendrobium orchids

4 to 5 stems of white or blue hydrangea

1 bunch of curly willow

Tall rectangle vase

Optional: LED lights, broken glass, rocks, clay tape

DESIGN TIP: Create an even bigger statement centerpiece by using leftover flowers from this recipe to create a matching low arrangement. Then place a few single stems in a bud vase next to the low arrangement so that you end up with a trio of matching arrangements in various sizes.

1 Place broken glass or LED lights at the bottom of the vase, if using. If you're using a small LED light, turn it on before putting it in the vase, since they usually last 24 hours. To secure the light to the bottom of the vase, use clay tape, or cover it with rocks or glass to hold it down. Fill the vase three-quarters full with water.

2 Prep all the flowers.

3 Cut the curly willow so it's about double the height of the vase. Angle 3 to 4 stems of curly willow inside the vase, with the bottom of the stems halfway down the vase. The bottom of the stems should be on the left side of the vase, with the stems angling across to rest on the right rim of the vase. Angle 3 to 4 more stems in the other direction, with the bottom of the stems on the right side and angled to the left. The stems will crisscross inside the vase. If some of the willow starts to fall down further into the vase, lift and prop it back up. You'll have to adjust all the stems in the vase as you keep adding them in.

4 Add in 3 to 4 more pieces of curly willow in the middle of the vase pointed straight up and down. If they sink down, pull them up a bit.

5 Cut the delphinium a few inches shorter than the curly willow. Insert the delphinium in the same way you added the willow, with the stems angled in and the blooms leaning against the opposite rim of the vase. You may not use all the stems. Turn the arrangement to make sure it's even.

6 Give the orchids a small cut on a slant and place throughout the outer part of the arrangement, leaning against the delphinium.

7 Cut the hydrangeas to about 5" to 6" long. Place them around the top of the vase so that they create a collar around the rim. This will also support the rest of the stems.

8 Make sure the arrangement is circular. Pull up any stems that may have dropped down. The bottom of all the stems should end halfway down the vase.

CARE TIP: If you make an arrangement the day before a party, you'll notice the water in the vase is dirty the next day. Usually we flush out the water under a faucet. But really large arrangements such as this one won't fit under the faucet. So change out the water by gently tilting the vase in the sink, pushing aside the flowers to make space, and emptying out the water. Fill the vase with fresh water from a hose or a watering can.

FESTIVE AND FUN

Bursting with bright colors, the yellows and reds of this design would fit right in at a fiesta or an outdoor summer get-together—any event where people can kick back and party!

    This is a little trickier to make because it's so tall. And because a fluted vase has a larger opening, it requires a lot of flowers to fill it. You also don't want to create something top-heavy, as then the vase can tip over. So if the vase is lighter than the weight of the flowers, you'll need to add rocks or something heavy to weigh it down.

PREP TIME: 15 minutes   COOK TIME: 40 minutes   SEASON: Year round   DIFFICULTY: 3   COST: $$$–$$$$

INGREDIENTS

1 bunch of orange or pink snapdragons

1 bunch of red or bright pink medium-stemmed roses (or 6 roses)

1 bunch of yellow or purple tulips

1 bunch of yellow mini calla lilies

1 bunch of yellow freesia

1 bunch of hanging amaranthus

Fluted vase

Optional: decorative aluminum wire (copper or silver), curly willow, rocks, ribbon

1 Prep all the flowers and separate into piles by type of flower.

2 If using, cut a foot or two of the wire, then bunch it up slightly and submerge the wire inside the vase. Fill the vase halfway with water.

3 Cut ½" off the bottom of the snapdragons and place the bunch near the back of the vase.

4 Cut the roses to about 8" long. Place 3 in a line against the front of the vase. Place the other 3 roses in a cluster above the first roses.

5 Give the tulips a small cut on the slant. Place the tulips in a cluster behind the roses on the left side of the vase, then lift them up to spread them out, making sure that the stems are in water.

6 Cut the calla lilies to about 8" long. Place the callas to the right of the roses, gently bending them to curve right and outward.

7 Cut the freesia to about 10" long. Place the freesia leaning to the right, directly behind the callas. Pull them up and out if they sink down.

8 Place the amaranthus stems deep inside the vase, at the front left of the vase, in front of the roses. The amaranthus can drape over the vase to rest on the table, or be cut shorter, depending on your preference.

the flower chef

SUNSET PALETTE

We have all kinds of artists on both sides of my family. My Nana Peggy was an amazing painter, my mother can draw well, and my brother is an incredibly talented photographer and fine artist. The list goes on and on! In many ways, I think of flower arranging as another type of painting, swirling together tones and textures of petals and stems to create a visual canvas. This arrangement, with its glorious oranges and yellows, is meant to capture the colors of a sunset over the beach—and is a nod to my family of artists.

This is one of my signature arrangements, and it looks a lot more expensive than it is. While cymbidium and phalaenopsis orchids are expensive, you can get bunches (10 stems) of thin-stemmed orchids like dendrobium or mokara for fairly cheap, and they're readily available—you just have to ask.

PREP TIME: **10 minutes** COOK TIME: **15 minutes** SEASON: **Year round** DIFFICULTY: **2** COST: **$$**

INGREDIENTS

1 bunch of white mini calla lilies

1 bunch of orange/yellow mokara orchids

1 bunch of yellow freesia

Thin gold or silver wire

White pebbles

Medium rectangle vase

DESIGN TIP: For a bolder variation on this recipe, switch out the white mini calla lilies and freesia for a single bunch each of orange spray roses and solidaster, then add a stem of red anthurium. Also, you can get about three small-to-medium arrangements out of this version by dividing up the flowers and using slightly smaller vases.

1 Prep all the flowers.

2 Add a 1" layer of pebbles to the bottom of the vase. Trim one orchid stem so that the topmost bloom will sit halfway below the top of the vase. Place the stem deep inside the rocks, then add in another ½" layer of rocks to fully anchor it. Fill the vase three-quarters full with water.

3 Secure the calla lilies with wire, halfway down the stems. Cut the stems to about 6" long and place at a slight angle inside the vase, with the blooms leaning against the front right corner.

4 Secure 3 to 4 stems of the orchids with wire, halfway down the stems. Cut the orchids to about 6" long and place at a slight angle inside the vase, behind the calla lilies, with the blooms leaning against the middle of the left side of the vase.

5 Secure the freesia with wire, halfway down the stems. Cut the stems to about 6" long and place at a slight angle inside the vase, with the blooms leaning against the back right corner of the vase. This is a bit of a balancing act, so adjust accordingly.

DESIGN TIP: This arrangement works well in a tapered vase, which is narrower on the top than the bottom (opposite of the fluted vase). The narrow opening will hold the bunches of flowers in place.

HIPPIE VASE

This retro-looking arrangement was inspired by the 1960s, with its psychedelic colors and its peace-loving, anything-goes vibe. Eye-popping magentas and tangerine oranges play with lime green, and everything comes together in a messy, fun, groovy mix. Definitely not a gift for a minimalist, this arrangement would be right-on for your favorite bohemian friend, or to make for a casual party. Fondue anyone?

PREP TIME: 10 minutes   COOK TIME: 30 minutes   SEASON: Year round   DIFFICULTY: 4   COST: $$–$$$

INGREDIENTS

1 bunch of purple dendrobium orchids

1 bunch of Bells of Ireland

1 bunch of white anemones

1 bunch of orange ranunculus

6" square vase

1 Wrap a few stems of orchids around your hand and place inside the vase. Fill the vase three-quarters full with water.

2 Cut the Bells of Ireland to about 12" long. Remove the flowers from the bottom third of each stem.

3 Choose 4 stems of bells that have the most prominent curve. Place a stem in each corner of the vase, making sure they're inside the ring of orchids and not caught between the orchids and the vase. Bend each stem in its natural direction to create an upside-down U shape, securing the top of each stem into the diagonally opposite corner, tucked inside the vase. [a]

4 You'll use 2 more stems of bells to create a collar that rests on the rim of the vase. Start with one stem of bells. Place one end in the back right corner, then circle the stem around the rim of the vase. Tuck the last 2" to 3" of the stem inside the edge of the vase. Take the second stem of bells, place it inside the vase where the first stem ended, then also circle that around the rim of the vase. Make sure the ends of the stems are tucked securely into the vase.

5 Cut the remaining orchid stems in half, removing the bottom blossoms to create a longer stem. Place evenly throughout the arrangement, in between the bells and along the outer edge of the vase.

6 Prep the anemones and give them a short cut on a slant. Place the stems evenly throughout the arrangement.

7 Prep and cut the ranunculus to about the length of the anemones and place evenly throughout the arrangement so that everything feels balanced.

CHAMPAGNE AND CAVIAR

Classy, fancy, and eminently elegant, this arrangement looks like you're serving champagne and caviar—and spent the money to match on your flowers. But looks are deceiving here. None of the flowers are expensive, and they're all easy to find.

This is an arrangement that demonstrates one of my design maxims: It's not what kind of flowers you're using, but how you arrange them that matters. In this case, I took inexpensive flowers and placed them just so in a really nice vase, proving that any flowers can look upscale when you artfully arrange them.

PREP TIME: **10 minutes**　COOK TIME: **15 minutes**　SEASON: **Year round**　DIFFICULTY: **2**　COST: **$$**

INGREDIENTS

1 bunch of purple or pink alstroemeria

1 bunch of red tulips

1 bunch of blue or purple irises

Half a bunch of bear grass

Silver ice bucket or medium silver vase

1 Prep the flowers and cut the stems so that they're all 6" to 8" taller than the vase. Force the irises open by pinching the tops of the flowers.

2 Place half the alstroemeria stems evenly throughout the outer edges of the arrangement.

3 Trim the other half of the alstroemeria 2" shorter and place in the middle of the arrangement.

4 Place 3 to 4 tulips together on each side (left and right) of the vase, toward the back.

5 Place the remaining tulips, 2 to 3 stems, toward the front right.

6 Place clusters of irises throughout the middle of the arrangement, breaking up the color.

7 Take the bear grass, cutting off an inch straight across the bottom, and insert the ends on the back left side between the flowers and the vase, deep in the arrangement. Bend the grass, forming an arch, and bring it forward, placing the top ends deep into the vase on the left side of the vase. Refer to Rainbow Love (page 122) for this technique. If a few strands pop out, you can gently pull them out and remove them, or leave them sticking out.

CARE TIP: I use alstroemeria as the filler flower, which lasts about 2 weeks. The tulips and irises wilt faster, but changing the water frequently will increase their longevity. This arrangement actually looks better over time, as the flowers bloom, open up, and lift up and outward.

freehand arrangements

PRETTY AS A PITCHER

Pitchers can give flowers a mod country feel or can make an arrangement look homey and quaint, depending on their pattern and style. Discount home stores are a good place to find cute, inexpensive pitchers for yourself or to give to friends.

You can use a variety of flowers for this arrangement, or keep it simple with one or two flowers that have a similar shape. If you go with a heavily patterned pitcher, I'd recommend sticking to one color of flower, so that the overall effect of your arrangement doesn't get too busy. In my recipe, the kelly green brightens up the muted peach, giving it a vibrant kick. If you want to keep the palette neutral, use eucalyptus instead, which also has a soothing fragrance that you'll find in most spas.

PREP TIME: 5 minutes   **COOK TIME:** 5 minutes   **SEASON:** Year round   **DIFFICULTY:** 1   **COST:** $

INGREDIENTS

1 bunch of Bells of Ireland

1 to 2 bunches of peach stock

Ceramic pitcher vase

1 Fill the pitcher three-quarters full with water. Prep all the flowers.

2 Cut the Bells of Ireland so they're double the height of the vase. Place the bells in the pitcher.

3 Give the stock stems a small cut on a slant.

4 Place the stock evenly throughout the vase, facing outward. Turn the pitcher midway through arranging to ensure that the flowers are balanced, pulling out any stems that are too closely clustered together. Reinsert them elsewhere in the arrangement.

8

CREATIVE DESIGNS

In this chapter, you'll take many of the techniques you've learned and tie them all together. Using wine bottles in gift arrangements, suspending orchids in a globe, making a garden basket entwined with flowers—now that you know the basics of design, you can play around and experiment, making incredible, elaborate arrangements with ease. Have fun getting creative!

GLITTER FEST

Kids love to glitter and decorate, which makes this the perfect arrangement for a children's birthday party. You can add glitter to just one flower for a slight hint of sparkle, or to most of the blooms, as many kids will prefer, for lots of shine. A note of caution: Glitter is fun, but it tends to go everywhere. I'd recommend making these arrangements outside or on a kitchen table—away from rugs and upholstery.

The mums used in this recipe go by many names: Kermit mums, pompom mums, and button mums. They're very hardy and will last for weeks. You can use clear glue to add glitter to the roses, or if you don't have any on hand, use egg whites instead. Though I use a thermos here, you can make this arrangement in a lunchbox (just put a layer of foam inside) by doubling the recipe.

the flower chef

PREP TIME: 15 minutes **COOK TIME:** 10 minutes **SEASON:** Year round **DIFFICULTY:** 1 **COST:** $$

INGREDIENTS

3 stems of hot pink roses

1 bunch of green button mums (or 3 to 4 stems)

1 bunch of yellow freesia

1 bunch of pink tulips (or 3 to 4 stems)

Clear glue or egg whites

Paper plates

Silver glitter

Thermos

1 Prep the flowers and cut all the stems to about 6" long. Fill the thermos three-quarters full with water.

2 Spread clear glue or egg whites on a paper plate. Put a pile of glitter on another paper plate. Dip each rose head lightly into the glue [a] and then into the glitter [b], as if you're breading chicken. Lightly shake off any excess glitter [c]. Set the roses on a clean paper plate so that the blooms hang off the edge. Dry for 10 minutes.

3 Place the mums in clusters evenly throughout the outer edges of the thermos, so the flowers are leaning against the edge.

4 Place 2 roses in the middle of the arrangement and have the third rose resting on the rim of the vase. Each rose should have room around it so that it can breathe.

5 Insert the freesia in clusters of 2 to 3 stems, evenly balanced throughout the arrangement.

6 Fill in any empty spaces with the tulips, angling them outward.

DESIGN TIP: Experiment to discover the color combinations you like best. Some of my favorites are: yellow/pink, plum/light green, bright red/burnt orange, and bright yellow/light green.

A FINE WINE

Wandering the aisles of a thrift store one afternoon, I happened across an ice bucket and used it to create an arrangement for a friend's birthday, tucking a bottle of wine inside. If your friend doesn't drink or you want a lusher floral effect, go ahead and fill the entire bucket with flowers. You can use an inexpensive plastic ice bucket if you're aiming for a more casual look, or try a fancy silver one for a special occasion. This is a thoughtful gift for anyone who loves wine, and makes a pretty centerpiece with or without the bottle.

PREP TIME: 20 minutes **COOK TIME: 15 minutes** **SEASON: Year round** **DIFFICULTY: 2** **COST: $$**

INGREDIENTS

3 to 4 bunches of various red, pink, or white flowers (dendrobium or mokara orchids, coxcomb, gerbera daisies, lisianthus, roses)

1 block of floral foam

Red floral spray paint

Ice bucket

Optional: bottle of wine or champagne

1 Prep all the flowers, then lay them down on newspaper outside. Spray the flowers with red floral spray paint. Let them dry for 10 minutes.

2 Soak the floral foam and place half the block in the bottom of the bucket. Stack the other half on top so that the foam is close to reaching the top of the bucket. If you're adding a bottle of wine or champagne to the bucket, wedge the wine bottle inside the bucket against the foam, if there's room. If there isn't room, carve out a chunk of foam the diameter of the bottle and a third of the depth, then slide the bottle into that space, angled outward.

3 Cut all the flowers to about 6" to 7" long. Place the flowers evenly throughout the foam, working from the outside in and clustering a few by type. Insert flowers around the wine so they cover part of the bottle.

DESIGN TIP: If you're using a simple bucket with a handle, spruce up the handle with ribbon, beads, lace, or whatever pretty materials you have on hand.

179

creative designs

GOTH FLOWERS

With its black vase and the deep, dark reds of the blooms, this arrangement is Tim Burtonesque—elegantly quirky, with an edge. It could be a perfect gift for a friend who has a more modern style. Or it would also be really nice for an upscale affair, set in an entranceway under a spotlight for maximum dramatic impact. Or for one of my favorite holidays, Halloween!

PREP TIME: **20 minutes**   COOK TIME: **35 minutes**   SEASON: **Year round**   DIFFICULTY: **3**   COST: **$$$**

INGREDIENTS

1 bunch of dark red roses ('Black Magic' or 'Black Baccara') (or 12 to 18 stems)

1 bunch of plum or black dahlias

1 bunch of black mini calla lilies

1 to 2 bunches of seasonal dark red flowers (coxcomb, chocolate cosmos, black hellebores, black pansies)

1 bunch of black ti leaves (or 4 to 5 leaves)

2 blocks of floral foam

Medium ceramic rectangle vase (black)

1 Soak the floral foam. Place the blocks in the vase to fill it to the top.

2 Prep and cut all the flowers to about 8" to 10" long.

3 Place the roses almost in a dome shape, clustered in the right half of the vase.

4 Insert a cluster of 4 to 5 dahlias in the front left corner, allowing them to be slightly stacked and overlapped. Insert another cluster of 3 to 4 dahlias toward the back right corner.

5 Place a cluster of 3 calla lilies in the front right corner, and another in the front left, both extending a few inches out from the vase. Add the rest of the callas in clusters of 2 to 3 evenly throughout the arrangement, making sure the blooms sit a little lower than the roses and dahlias.

6 Fill in the empty spaces with the remaining red flowers, keeping 2 to 3 stems clustered together in various spots of the arrangement. You may not need to use all of the flowers. All of the flowers should be at slightly varying heights for a textured look.

7 Fold the ti leaves in half, shiny side out, and insert both ends (the point and the stem) along the front edge of the vase. Since they're smaller and thinner than regular green ti leaves, they bend easily and you don't need to remove the vein. You can also curl and staple the leaves using the technique from the Holiday Sparkle recipe (page 204).

DESIGN TIP: Like almost all the other recipes, the ingredients here don't have to be exact—but since the overall color is important to replicating the look, just make sure that whatever flowers you substitute are dark red. I'll often use dyed real flowers if I can't find the color blooms I need, but artificial flowers can be arranged beautifully too, so definitely do experiment with them if you're so inclined or if you can't find the deep reds in this arrangement. You can always use a mix of dried, fake, and sprayed flowers.

GLIMMERING GLOBE

Twinkly, sparkly, and unusual, this is the kind of arrangement that would be perfect for a New Year's Eve celebration with champagne or for a splashy awards event. The flower blooms appear to be floating underwater, and the bullion wire makes it shimmer. It's also a good one for large celebrations because you can make lots of them all at once.

You can create a vertical version in glass cylinders, layering the wire and orchids on top of each other. Roses work equally well in this design, and red roses and gold wire look especially glamorous.

A quick warning: This is a very heavy arrangement, so if you're traveling with it, only fill the vase one-quarter full with water and then add in the remaining water with a watering can once you have it in its final location.

PREP TIME: **20 minutes**   COOK TIME: **15 minutes**   SEASON: **Year round**   DIFFICULTY: **2**   COST: **$**

INGREDIENTS

1 stem of phalaenopsis orchid (can be cut from a plant), 6 to 8 blooms

Spool of 24-gauge gold metallic wire

Spool of 28-gauge silver bullion wire

Medium bubble bowl

DESIGN TIP: You can also illuminate this arrangement with an LED light. Turn on the light before adding the wire, then secure it to the bottom of the vase with clay tape.

1 Cut the blooms off the orchid.

2 Cut about a 2'-long piece of the 24-gauge gold metallic wire. Thread the wire through the center of each orchid bloom, as if you're making a necklace or a lei.

3 Push down each bloom so they're about 3" to 5" apart on the wire. After you push down each orchid, create a small bend in the wire to hold it in place. Once all the blooms are wired, set the orchids aside. [a]

4 Cut a 3'-long piece of silver bullion wire. Lightly scrunch the wire, then gently tease it apart to create a loose, fluffy ball. This wire will add an ethereal, delicate look to the arrangement, and keep the wired orchids in place once they're submerged.

5 Place the bunched-up ball of wire inside the vase, pulling it apart even more if needed to fill out the bubble bowl. Cut another piece of bullion wire to bunch up and insert into the bowl if the bowl doesn't look full enough. Fill the bowl three-quarters full with water.

6 Loop the wired orchids inside the circumference of the vase, between the vase and the bullion wire. Be sure to flip the orchids so they face out. [b] If you have any extra orchid blooms, insert them into the middle of the arrangement, nested deep within the bullion wire to keep them in place and prevent them from floating to the top.

DESIGN TIP: Place the spool of bullion wire in a small vase while unraveling. This will make it easier to handle and keep the wire in one spot.

FLOWER LATTICE

It's so calming to walk by a garden and see ivy and flowers wending their way up a wooden lattice or open fence, the blooms twining in a delicate burst of colors and textures. This design replicates that garden look, using curly willow and whatever flowers you like, in an arrangement that's just right for an afternoon tea, a picnic, or a kids' party. Because it's meant to look natural, this is a good recipe for leftover flowers; simply mix and match whatever flowers you have on hand. It would also look pretty to make this just with tulips, especially in the spring when it's raining and you want something cheery indoors.

You can make this by yourself, which is what I do, but it is easier to have one person hold the curly willow while another person secures it with wire.

PREP TIME: 15 minutes   **COOK TIME:** 40 minutes   **SEASON:** Spring/Summer/Fall   **DIFFICULTY:** 4   **COST:** $$

INGREDIENTS

1 bunch of purple campanula (or 3 to 4 stems)

1 bunch of pink tulips (or 3 to 4 stems)

1 bunch of snapdragons (or 3 to 4 stems)

Optional: leftover closed flowers (lilies, peonies, freesia)

Sheet moss

1 bunch of curly willow

2 pieces of 18"-long 22- to 24-gauge green straight wire

1 block of floral foam

Round plastic dish

1 Soak the foam. Cut it in half horizontally and place it inside the dish, trimming the foam so that it's even with the top of the dish. Fill in any remaining spaces with small pieces of foam. The foam should fit snugly and fill the entire dish.

2 Prep the flowers. They can all be trimmed to various heights between 12" to 16" long, so that they look natural and like they're growing out of the moss. Keep 2 to 3 stems of the campanula long and place them in the middle of the dish.

3 Place a few stems of tulips and snapdragons on either side of the campanula.

4 Cut 1 to 2 stems of each type of flower about 3" long and insert them as 2 clusters in the middle of the arrangement, both in front of and behind the taller flowers.

5 Using curly willow, we're going to make a lattice for the flowers. To do this, cut 2 pieces of willow about 14" to 18" long, so that they're a few inches taller than the campanula. Place the willow vertically in the foam on either side of the taller flowers.

6 Cut 4 pieces of wire, each about 6" long, and set within easy reach.

7 Cut 4 more pieces of curly willow, each about 12" to 14" long, so they're a few inches longer than the diameter of the plastic dish. Stretch a piece of willow horizontally across either side of the taller flowers, about halfway down the stems, so that they're sandwiched between the two pieces of willow. Tie both ends of the willow together using the wire, binding them like a twist tie. Cut off any excess wire.

8 Repeat step 7 with the other two pieces of willow, again sandwiching the taller flowers, this time right below the blooms.

9 Lightly wet a piece of sheet moss and gently stretch it out. Cover any visible foam with moss, tucking the moss over the sides of the foam. The moss should stay in place, but you can also use wire to pin and secure the moss into the foam, as described in the Roses and Grass recipe (page 74).

GARDEN BASKET

If you group flowers tight and low in a basket, you get a polished, classy, outdoorsy look, instead of a frumpy and dated basket arrangement. Depending on your preferred aesthetic, you can try different styles. For a country basket, use fresh hydrangea blooms with lisianthus and waxflower draping over the sides. For an English garden look, use taller flowers like larkspur and delphinium.

This recipe is for a more traditional garden basket design. You can secure moss to the handle or outer edge of the basket using thin gold wire. If you have a basket without a handle, you can create one of your own. Simply attach curly willow (you can braid it together or use multiple pieces bundled next to each other) to one end and arch the branches over to the other side, securing it to the basket with wire.

PREP TIME: **25 minutes**   COOK TIME: **20 minutes**   SEASON: **Year round**   DIFFICULTY: **2**   COST: **$$–$$$**

INGREDIENTS

1 bunch of sunflowers

1 bunch of orange and/or yellow roses (or 10 to 10 stems)

1 bunch of orange spray roses

Optional: 1 bunch of red or yellow coxcomb, tulips, ranunculus

Spanish moss (can use sheet or mood moss too)

1 block of floral foam

Spool of 24-gauge metallic wire (any color)

Basket with plastic liner

1 Soak the floral foam and cut it to fill the plastic liner. If the foam doesn't reach the top of the liner, that's OK; just make sure to securely insert each flower into the foam.

2 Place a 3"- to 4"-wide piece of moss over the basket handle. Loop wire over and around the moss and handle, securing the moss to the basket. Keep adding moss, looping wire around it as you go, until the entire handle is covered in moss. You can also add moss to only part of the handle or basket, if you prefer.

3 Take more moss and place it around the rim of the basket, tucking one end deep into the basket and letting the other end of the moss slightly drape over the basket edge.

4 Prep the flowers and cut them all to about 6" long.

5 Place the sunflowers evenly throughout the basket.

6 Add in the roses evenly throughout the basket. They should be inserted into the foam so that they're the same height as the sunflowers that sit toward the outer edges of the arrangement, and left a bit taller in the center so that they're more visible.

7 Fill in the empty spaces between the roses and sunflowers with the spray roses. If you're using additional flowers, add them into the arrangement, keeping the flower heads at a fairly uniform height.

FIVE-STAR CANDELABRA

This isn't an everyday recipe but is intended for when you feel inspired to go big—say for a holiday party or a wedding. That said, you're basically just putting flowers in foam in a plastic dish, so it's a lot easier than it looks.

To make it, you first fill a plastic dish with foam, add flowers, and then attach the finished arrangement to the candelabra. You can use this technique with decorative vases of any size that can't hold water, as long as the plastic dish is the same diameter as the vase to which it's being secured. Traditionally, florists will wrap the foam and plastic dish together with chicken wire to prevent the foam from crumbling if too many stems are added, but I've never had a problem using just the foam and floral tape. Chicken wire can be a pain to work with because it is sharp and cumbersome to store.

PREP TIME: 20 minutes   COOK TIME: 40 minutes   SEASON: Year round   DIFFICULTY: 3   COST: $$$$

INGREDIENTS

7 to 8 stems of antique green hydrangea

1 bunch of orange spray roses or dinner plate dahlias

1 bunch of orange ranunculus

1 bunch of orange tulips

Candelabra

4" to 6" round plastic dish, the same diameter as the center of the candelabra

1 block of floral foam

Thick green floral tape

Clay tape

1 bunch of hanging foliage: ivy, jasmine, or any seasonal hanging vine (or can cut directly from a potted plant)

CARE TIP: When making the arrangement, place the plastic dish on top of an upside-down bucket or crate on the table when you're inserting the flowers. It is better for your back to work this way if you're standing up.

1 Soak the foam, cut it in half horizontally, and add the block to the dish. Fill in any remaining spaces with small pieces of foam. The foam should fit snugly and fill the entire dish. Stretch multiple strips of floral tape around the dish and the foam, crisscrossing as you go so that the strips make a cross or a star shape over the top of the foam to hold it in. See Branch Out (page 100) for a photo.

2 Prep all the flowers.

3 Cut the hydrangeas to about 8" long, and place them evenly throughout until the arrangement starts to take on a dome shape and looks fairly symmetrical. All the other flowers will be pushed into and through the hydrangea blooms and into the foam.

4 Trim about ¼" off the bottom of the spray roses, leaving as much length as possible. Place clusters of 2 to 3 stems evenly throughout the arrangement.

5 Trim about ¼" off the bottom of the ranunculus and place them in clusters of 2 to 3 stems evenly throughout the arrangement, pointed outward.

6 Place clusters of 2 to 3 tulips evenly throughout the arrangement, angled outward.

7 Put the clay tape on top of the candelabra, gently pressing down so that it is secure, then carefully and firmly place the plastic dish with flowers on top of it.

8 Take a few steps back and look at the candelabra, making sure it looks even and balanced. Pull out any flowers to fill out the shape, or add extra flowers to any empty spaces. The flowers should extend out over the entire candelabra stand.

9 To soften the arrangement and give it a romantic feel, we'll accent it with vines all the way around the arrangement. Cut the vine into pieces that are 18" to 24" long. Insert the end of one vine stem (ivy, in this case) into the foam, tucked under the flowers. Drape the ivy so it hangs slightly below the flowers, then tuck the other end of the stem into the foam. Repeat with a couple more vines, so that the vines hang in low loops all the way around the arrangement.

DESIGN TIP: If there are still empty spaces when you're finished arranging, push the flower stems in deeper to bring the entire arrangement closer together.

SUBMERGED FLOWERS

For a clean, modern, elegant look, submerging entire flowers underwater never goes out of fashion. There are various ways to submerge them—the technique you use depends on the type of flower you're working with. For thin stems like mini calla lilies, dendrobium orchids, and tulips, you can use a frog pin (secured to the bottom of the vase with clay tape), or tape the flowers together with clear floral tape and hold down the stems with rocks. You can line the bottom of the vase with a ti leaf to hide the frog pin, rocks, or stems. Thick stems, like cymbidium orchids, are usually the width of the vase and will stay in place on their own.

Although this design looks simple, it actually takes some time to do. Getting the flowers to face out and cutting them the perfect height often requires many attempts.

Prep time: 15 minutes COOK TIME: **30 minutes** SEASON: **Year round** DIFFICULTY: **4** COST: **$$–$$$**

INGREDIENTS

1 bunch of white tulips (or 3 stems)

1 bunch of white dendrobium orchids (or 3 to 5 stems)

1 bunch of large white calla lilies (or 3 stems)

Rocks

Clear floral tape

3 cylinder vases (short, medium, tall)

DESIGN TIP: You can submerge almost any type of flower. Some of my favorites to submerge are ruscus, baby's breath, hydrangeas, cymbidium orchids, and roses.

1 Prep all the flowers.

2 For each vase, add a ½" layer of rocks.

3 Trim one tulip stem so that the top of the bloom will sit just below the top of the shortest vase when the stem is inserted in the layer of rocks. You may have to measure and trim a couple times to get it right.

4 Cut one tulip stem an inch shorter, and the other tulip 2" shorter than the tallest tulip. Secure all 3 tulips at the very bottom of the stems with the clear floral tape; you want them to look stacked, so that each tulip is a slightly different height.

5 Place the tulip stems deep into the rocks in the middle of the vase, making sure the flowers are facing out. Add in another ½" of rocks to secure the stems. Fill the vase to the top with water.

6 Repeat steps 3 to 5 with the dendrobium orchids in the medium vase. The orchid stems can all be the same height.

7 Repeat steps 3 to 5 with the calla lilies in the tallest vase, stacked in height like the tulips.

DESIGN TIP: Add a 1" to 3" floating candle on top of each arrangement to create a romantic centerpiece. Make sure the water is 1" to 2" below the top of the vase so that it doesn't spill over. Place one candle inside each vase and light the candles right before guests arrive.

creative designs

WHEAT GRASS GARDEN

Super-perky, vibrant, and fun, this versatile arrangement turns healthy wheat grass into an eye-catcher for your table. Suitable for all kinds of occasions, you can use it for an escort card table at a wedding, as a pretty entrance piece at a party, for a bar mitzvah, a baby shower, Easter brunch...you name it! You can buy flats of wheat grass from high-end grocers or at the flower mart. It doesn't live long—usually a week or so.

PREP TIME: 20 minutes   **COOK TIME:** 10 minutes   **SEASON:** Year round   **DIFFICULTY:** 1   **COST:** $$$–$$$$

INGREDIENTS

1 flat of wheat grass

1 bunch of pink gerbera daisies (or 6 to 7 stems)

1 bunch of pink tulips (or 3 to 5 stems)

1 bunch of orange tulips (or 3 to 5 stems)

1 bunch of yellow tulips (or 2 to 3 stems)

1 bunch of purple anemones (or 4 to 5 stems)

1 bunch of billy balls

18 to 25 water tubes (one for each stem used)

Wood rectangle box with liner

CARE TIP: Place filled water tubes upright in a piece of foam so you can grab them easily while arranging.

1 Cut the wheat grass to fit the size of the box, so that the entire box is filled with the grass.

2 Fill the water tubes with water. Prep the flowers and cut all the stems to about 6" long, except for the gerbera daisies, which should be cut to about 4" to 5" long. Place each stem in a water tube.

3 Place the pointy ends of each water tube into the roots of the grass, so that every flower stands up straight. Insert the flowers evenly throughout, until the arrangement looks balanced.

4 Place the billy balls evenly throughout, pushing the stems directly into the roots of the grass. You can press some of the stems in the front deeper into the grass for varying heights.

DESIGN TIP: Other blooms that would work well in the Wheat Grass Garden arrangement are sunflowers, poppies, and common daisies.

PRETTY POTTED ORCHID

Potted orchids in floral shops always look so pretty, fluffed up with moss and arranged in gorgeous containers. But those orchids are often quite expensive; one place where I used to work charged $75 for an orchid that could be found at the flower mart for just $12. So why pay the higher price? Instead, get an inexpensive orchid and easily transform it into a pricey-looking gift by adding your own moss and container.

Since orchid blooms last 2 to 3 months, most people will toss the orchid after the blooms have fallen off. If you continue to care for it, however, the orchid will bloom again the following year. Just repot it with soil. Although I don't have a green thumb—people often assume I'm a gardener, but I promise you, I've managed to kill the hardiest ivy and succulents—even I can keep these orchids alive.

PREP TIME: **5 minutes**   COOK TIME: **10 minutes**   SEASON: **Year round**   DIFFICULTY: **1**   COST: **$–$$**

INGREDIENTS

1 potted phalaenopsis orchid

Mood moss

Curly willow

River rocks or pebbles

Twine or raffia

Filler: e.g., newspaper, bubble wrap

6" to 8" square ceramic vase

DESIGN TIP: To mix up the look of this design, you can place the orchid in a square glass vase and fill with sand in between the container and vase, you can fill the pot with moss, you can add shells...you can basically do anything you want!

1 Place the potted orchid in the center of the vase. Surround the pot with filler to hold it in place. The orchid pot should be even with the top of the vase. If it's too low, place filler underneath, making sure the pot is secure.

2 Remove the plastic clips that secure the orchid to the stick holding it upright, replacing the clips with small loops of twine. Trim the excess twine after tying it in a bow or knot.

3 Place a few stems of curly willow deep in the orchid pot, tying it to the orchid stem with twine to hold the willow in place. Trim the willow to the desired height.

4 Lightly wet the mood moss and wring it out. Place the moss on top of the vase so that it completely covers the orchid pot and filler.

5 Top the moss with a handful of river rocks or pebbles.

CARE TIP: While the orchid is blooming, mist the petals lightly with water every few days and keep it out of direct sunlight. Carefully water the plant with a half cup of water every 7 to 10 days. Note that overwatering will kill it. When the orchid flowers fall off (within 1 to 3 months after blooming), you can cut the stem about a third of the way up from the base, where the stem has turned brown, and repot it. Continue to water as you would if it were blooming, and it should bloom again the next year.

creative designs

REFLEXED ROSES

Reflexed roses look more lush and romantic than regular roses. They're also a little exotic, and even sensual, since you're bending the petals back to display their inner surface—a look that enhances the color and changes the shape of the blooms. Reflexed roses also take up more physical space, since a reflexed rose is 2 to 3 times as big as a single regular rose, and are therefore better when you're on a budget. This is a great go-to recipe for any occasion. Even people who don't normally like roses will love this look.

To reflex roses, you gently bend the petals back and downward. It will shorten the longevity of the flowers by a few days, but that's OK since this technique works well with older roses—it's like using stale bread to make croutons. The petals need to be soft and pliable enough to bend back (they will break if you use fresh roses). Two-toned roses really make this design pop.

PREP TIME: 5 minutes   **COOK TIME:** 10 minutes   **SEASON:** Year round   **DIFFICULTY:** 1   **COST:** $

INGREDIENTS

1 bunch of roses (or 12 to 15 stems) (two-toned roses, such as Latin Lady or Fire and Ice, are ideal); roses that are a few days old are best

Small ceramic vase

DESIGN TIP: You can also reflex open tulips. The look will surprise you!

DESIGN TIP: You can use reflexed roses in any of the recipes with roses in the book. Cut the number of roses needed by a third or half, since reflexed roses take up more room.

1 Prep the roses and remove the thin, pointy greens surrounding the outer petals at the base of the roses. This is really the only time I remove them.

2 Take an outer petal between your thumb and your index and middle fingers, then gently and slowly bend the petal back (pushing up on the petal with your thumb and carefully pulling with your fingers) so that it's almost inverted. [a]

3 Repeat with all the petals, going in a circle and working your way toward the center of the bloom. Stop when the petals become too small to pull back. Blow in the center of the rose to slightly open the center petals more. [b–c]

4 Repeat with all the other roses.

5 Fill the vase three-quarters full with water.

6 Cut the rose stems to about 5" to 6" long. Place the roses evenly throughout the vase, inserting roses around the outer edges and working toward the middle of the vase. The center roses should be slightly overlapping and resting lightly on the outer roses.

7 Fill in any empty spaces with the remaining stems. The design can be slightly asymmetrical.

TEXTURED ROSES

This arrangement is all about giving roses texture and dimension by placing them at different heights and pointing them in different directions—instead of by reflexing. The trick is to arrange the roses quickly so that the stems become almost entangled, which will hold them in place. You then pull out the stems, adjusting the height of the flowers to create the shape. You can mix two similar colors to create a subtle contrast, as I did with the peach and cream roses.

INGREDIENTS

1 bunch of very open white, cream, peach, or blush roses (or 14 to 16 roses)

Small ceramic vase

1 Prep the roses and cut the blooms to about 5" to 6" above the top of the vase.

2 Place the roses in the vase so that all the stems are crisscrossing. When all the roses are inside the vase, pull random rose blooms up an inch or two so that all the roses are at various heights and pointing in various directions.

HOLLYWOOD GLAM

Inspired by a Marilyn Monroe exhibit I saw at an art gallery, I set out to make an arrangement that included a subtle touch of Old Hollywood glamour and style. Browsing at a craft store soon after, I spotted an ethereal-looking feather boa and thought to myself: *That looks very Marilyn.* This would be a fabulous, lighthearted arrangement for an Academy Awards viewing party, or for any fun celebration or theme event.

You can cut a boa into many sections, but beware—the loose feathers get messy.

PREP TIME: **10 minutes** COOK TIME: **15 minutes** SEASON: **Year round** DIFFICULTY: **2** COST: **$–$$**

INGREDIENTS

3 stems of white hydrangea

1 bunch of cream or white roses
(or 6 to 7 stems)

1 white feather boa

Clear floral tape

5" to 6" square mirror or silver vase

1 With the tape, make a 3 x 3 grid over the opening of the vase, then fill the vase three-quarters full with water. Prep the flowers.

2 Cut the hydrangeas to 5" to 6" long and place them in the vase in a triangular shape so that two stems rest against the corners of the vase and the third rests against the opposite side.

3 Cut the roses to 5" long. Insert them evenly spaced through the hydrangeas.

4 Cut the boa to about 16" long. Tuck one end into a corner, then drape it diagonally over the flowers, looping it gently through the hydrangea and the roses. Trim any excess once you reach the opposite corner. Place the other end deep into the corner of the vase, so that it's secure.

creative designs

OMBRE FLOWERS

Ombre—when various shades of color slide into each other, going from light to dark—has become a very popular look, from hair to clothes to flowers. Although it's trendy, I also think it's a classic look for flower arrangements and relatively easy to achieve. In addition to staying within the shades of one color (pale pink to blush to hot pink), and neighboring colors (pink to red, yellow to orange, green to blue), you can do an ombre arrangement of rainbow colors or metallic colors (black to silver, gold to bronze). The modern pavé style keeps it compact and stylish, making an eye-catching centerpiece for a dinner party.

In this recipe, I use a 10" plastic dish, and about half the flowers from each bunch. For a longer arrangement appropriate for a dining room table, use a dish 14" to 16" long with two blocks of foam and the entire bunch of each type of flower.

PREP TIME: **10 minutes**   COOK TIME: **10 minutes**   SEASON: **Year round**   DIFFICULTY: **1**   COST: **$$$**

INGREDIENTS

6 to 7 bunches of various pink flowers in different shades (stock, roses, dahlias, lisianthus, spray roses, peonies)

2 blocks of floral foam

10" plastic rectangle dish

DESIGN TIP: Use a metallic plastic dish instead of the standard green so if the dish is exposed, it still looks glitzy.

1 Soak the floral foam and place it in the dish, trimming the top so that it's about even with the top of the dish.

2 Prep the flowers and cut all the stems to about 4" to 5" long.

3 Starting with the lightest pink flowers, insert them in a row along the right side of the vase (shown at the top in photo).

4 Continue with the next lightest shade, adding another row directly beside the first. Do the same with the rest of the flowers, adding rows that go from light to dark, creating single or double rows of flowers depending on the size of the blooms. The order shown here, going from light to dark, is: stock, spray roses, dahlias, lisianthus, spray roses, roses, peonies.

5 Adjust so that the flowers are all about the same height.

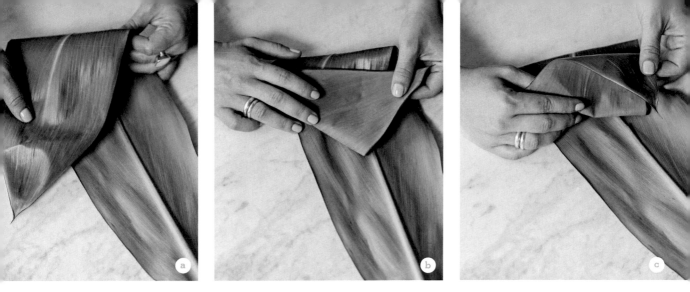

GRAFFITI LEAVES

Whether you love it or hate it, graffiti is an inevitable part of every cityscape. This arrangement is inspired by that out-of-the-box street art, and true to the DIY vibe of the medium, it was made with materials I already had on hand. This would be a good gift for someone who doesn't really like flowers—or for a friend who has a supercool downtown style.

PREP TIME: 15 minutes **COOK TIME:** 15 minutes **SEASON:** Year round **DIFFICULTY:** 2 **COST:** $

INGREDIENTS

1 to 2 bunches of ti leaves

Stapler

Clear floral tape

3 colors of spray paint (various neon shades)

DESIGN TIP: Create a funky but natural bouquet by making this same bouquet without spray-painting the leaves.

1 Lay down the ti leaves in a single layer on top of newspaper or trash bags outside. Spray the front and back of 2 to 3 leaves one color, then spray 2 to 3 more leaves another color, and then 2 to 3 leaves the third color. Let them dry for about 10 minutes.

2 Once the leaves are dry, fold each leaf by holding a stem and bending the top third of the leaf over 2 to 3 times like an accordion. You may hear it snap, which is OK. Once you bend and fold the top of the leaf a few times, staple the bunched-up part of the leaf 2 to 3 times, as close to the stem as possible. For a wider variety of shapes, bend some leaves in half. [a–c]

3 Make a horizontal cut on either side of the stem of the folded ti leaves (don't cut the stem). Then peel the bottom pieces of leaf off of the stem, leaving behind a long, bare ti leaf stem topped by the curl. See Holiday Sparkle (page 204) for this technique.

4 Secure all the leaves with clear floral tape to create a bouquet of various shades, or create a bunch of mini bouquets by gathering and taping the same-colored leaves together. Place them in a narrow vase or leave them standing upright.

CARE TIP: If the paint on the ti leaves cracks or chips when you're folding them, take them outside and touch them up with spray paint so they're fully covered in color.

HOLIDAY SPARKLE

Twinkly and with a dash of festive flair, simple ball ornaments are always fun to add to an arrangement. Though typically intended for the holidays, you could really use them all year round if you wish. Use whites and blues for Hanukkah or traditional green and red for Christmas. I like mixing deep purples and plums with silver for something more neutral, but even in this color palette, it's easy to experiment with tones, mixing and matching any purple or plum flowers to create your own look.

You'll often see curled ti leaves in more expensive arrangements. You can either insert them first, then add the flowers so that the leaves frame the flowers, or add the ti leaves afterward as accents.

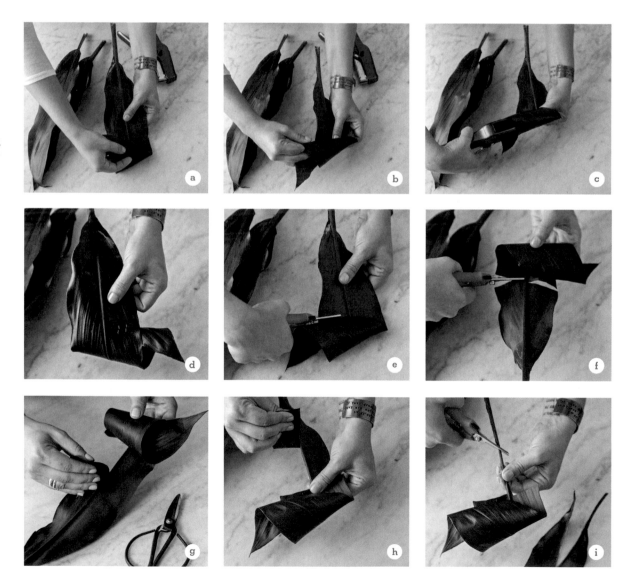

PREP TIME: 25 minutes   COOK TIME: 25 minutes   SEASON: Fall/Winter/Spring   DIFFICULTY: 3   COST: $$$$

INGREDIENTS

1 bunch of red or 'Black Baccara' roses (or 7 to 8 stems)

1 bunch of plum or black dahlias

1 bunch of purple anemones

1 bunch of black mini calla lilies (or 4 to 5 stems)

1 bunch of purple tulips (or 7 to 8 stems)

1 bunch of dusty miller

1 bunch of small black ti leaves

1 to 2 blocks of floral foam (depending on the size of the dish)

Stapler

10 small silver and gold ball ornaments with wires (if they don't come with wires, create small loops using floral wire)

Low silver rectangle dish (12" to 16" long) with liner

1 Soak the floral foam and place it in the dish. Cut the foam so that it's 1" above the top of the dish.

2 Prep all the flowers.

3 Wrap the top third of a ti leaf around your fingers to create a layered curl, making sure the shiny side is facing out. Staple the back of the curl so that you can't see the staple from the front. **[a–d]**

4 Below the curl, make a horizontal cut on either side of the stem (don't cut the stem). Then peel the bottom pieces of leaf off of the stem, leaving behind a long, bare ti leaf stem topped by the curl. Trim the stem to about 3" long. Repeat steps 3 and 4 with about 7 more leaves. **[e–i]**

5 Cut the roses to about 4" to 6" long. If the roses aren't fully bloomed, gently push them open and blow in the center so that they're as open as possible. Place clusters of roses evenly throughout the dish.

6 Cut the dahlias to 4" to 6" long, placing 2 to 3 blooms next to each other evenly throughout the arrangement.

7 Angle pairs of ti leaves evenly throughout the arrangement. A few can go in the corners.

8 Cut the anemones and calla lilies to about 4" to 6" long and place clusters of each nestled in by the ti leaves.

9 Cut the tulips to about 4" to 6" long, and place them throughout the arrangement near the ti leaves.

10 Add in the dusty miller evenly throughout, filling in any empty spaces.

11 Cut the ornament wires to 3" to 4" long. Place 3 clusters of ornaments toward the outer edges of the arrangement, nestled in between the flowers.

DESIGN TIP: The flowers in this arrangement should end up at slightly varying heights, creating an "in and out" type look that lends texture to the composition.

MIAMI LOVE

With its vibrant culture, amazing energy, and miles of beach, Miami feels like home to me. I love how the city blends beach culture with urban life, topped off with a Latin American influence. This arrangement was inspired by Miami Beach's Art Deco District, with its colors of white, blue, and coral. Since I couldn't find a flower in the shade of blue that I wanted, I used a vase in that shade instead.

This is such a cool arrangement because you can make it as small or as large as you want; it's very easy to scale. You could create a long and low arrangement by placing 3 to 4 vases next to each other and doubling or tripling the recipe.

PREP TIME: **10 minutes**   COOK TIME: **15 minutes**   SEASON: **Year round**   DIFFICULTY: **3**   COST: **$$–$$$**

INGREDIENTS

1 bunch of white mini calla lilies

1 bunch of white spider mums (or 4 to 5 stems)

1 bunch of orange, peach, or coral roses (or 5 to 6 stems)

1 bunch of orange or coral mini carnations

Thick green floral tape or rubber band

Small vase (blue)

1 Fill the vase three-quarters full with water. Prep the flowers and cut all the stems to about 10" long.

2 Spiral a bouquet using the calla lilies, mums, and roses.

3 Pull the carnations through so they're clustered near the roses. You may have to do this a few times to get the exact placement you want.

4 Secure the bouquet with thick green floral tape or a rubber band.

5 Cut the flower stems so that the blooms will rest on the rim of the vase. Place inside the vase.

creative des gns

MID-CENTURY MOD

My father is an antique dealer with a passion for mid-century modern antiques and furniture. With its clean lines punctuated by swoops and swirls, along with that era's naturalistic colors of orange, yellow, and green, this arrangement was inspired by that coolly casual aesthetic. This looks like it was lifted from the lobby of a Palm Springs hotel in the 1950s—can't you just picture Frank Sinatra strolling by?

PREP TIME: **20 minutes**   COOK TIME: **20 minutes**   SEASON: **Year round**   DIFFICULTY: **3**   COST: **$$**

INGREDIENTS

3 medium 4" succulents

2 small 2" succulents

1 bunch of black mini calla lilies (or 5 to 6 stems)

3 stems of yellow protea

2 stems of orange protea

5 pieces of 18"-long 20-gauge straight stem wire

Floral stem tape

1 block of floral foam

Ceramic rectangle vase (white or black)

1 Soak the foam and place the block vertically in the vase. It should take up the entire vase; if there's a lot of room around it, soak another block of foam and cut to fill the spaces in the vase.

2 Wire and tape the succulents to create fake stems, using the technique in steps 2 and 4 from Succulent Bouquet (page 53). Set them aside.

3 Trim an inch off of 3 to 4 calla lily stems, and place them in the back left corner of the vase. They should rise about 3" to 5" above the top of the vase.

4 Trim 2" to 3" off of 2 more callas and place them in the front right corner, inserting them into the foam so that they sit a bit lower than the callas in back.

5 Cut the proteas to 6" long. Place 2 yellow proteas toward the front left corner deep into the foam, so that the heads are resting on the rim of the vase. Place another yellow protea behind and to the right of the other ones at about the same height.

6 Place an orange protea in the front right corner, so that the head is resting on the rim of the vase. Place the other orange protea in the back center, higher than the rest, so that it rises about 6" to 7" above the top of the vase.

7 Place a medium succulent deep in the foam behind the 2 yellow proteas so that the succulent rests partially on top of them. Place another medium succulent in the back right corner, next to the orange protea, so that the succulent is resting on the rim of the vase. Place the last medium succulent in the middle of the back of the vase so that it rests on the edge.

8 Place the small succulents in the front of the vase between the yellow and orange proteas, slightly overlapping and resting on the rim of the vase.

GARLAND FLOWERS

Organically rustic looking, and beautiful with any table setting, garlands are very popular right now. They're easily adjusted to any size or length of table, and they can be customized to fit any theme or aesthetic. They make wonderful arrangements for weddings, banquets, holiday gatherings, or any other event where people will be seated at long tables.

Garlands are traditionally made by stringing flowers on wire—or using wire, chicken wire, and foam to tie bunches of flowers together. It's recently become trendy to use a garland as a table centerpiece. To do this, you can layer the foliage and flowers on top of and in between each other. It looks very impressive, but it's straightforward to make.

PREP TIME: 15 minutes   COOK TIME: 15 minutes   SEASON: Year round   DIFFICULTY: 1   COST: $$–$$$

INGREDIENTS

1 bunch of silver dollar or seeded eucalyptus

1 bunch of white flowers such as Star of Bethlehem or lisianthus

1 bunch of white or cream roses (or 6 to 12 stems)

2 to 3 larger 3" to 4" succulents

Optional: wood or balsa wood flowers, raw cotton (on stems sold through wholesalers and some craft stores)

1 Cut the eucalyptus into pieces 6" to 10" long (depending on the width of the table) and place them in an overlapping line down the center of the table, as if you're creating a table runner. The leaves should be fanned outward.

2 Prep the white flowers and the roses and cut them all to about 3" to 4" long, then place them evenly throughout the layer of eucalyptus. Tuck the stems in between the eucalyptus so they're hidden.

3 Remove the succulents from their containers, then clean off all the dirt, leaving just the small stem. Add the wood flowers and cotton, if you are using them, and the succulents evenly balanced down the length of the arrangement. Place the succulents on top of the eucalyptus, tucking in the stems.

CARE TIP: This is a striking (and simple) tablescape, but it only lasts for one night. If you want it to last an extra day or two, either put every flower in a water tube and conceal the tubes in the eucalyptus, or make a centerpiece with a plastic dish and floral foam.

creative designs

ON VACATION

My Pop Bernie encouraged me to create my own work. I find a lot of his traits in myself, including a love of movement and adventure. I was always a beach bum, even as a child, and this arrangement makes you feel like you're on vacation somewhere sunny and warm any time of year. Epitomizing my passion for nature and flowers, this arrangement is dedicated in his honor.

Eye-catching and outdoorsy, grapewood can be a wonderful décor element all by itself and is found in numerous craft and supply stores. This is a wonderfully flexible recipe, with endless variations and possibilities.

PREP TIME: 15 minutes   **COOK TIME:** 20 minutes   **SEASON:** Year round   **DIFFICULTY:** 2   **COST:** $–$$

INGREDIENTS

Mix of 7 flower stems (shown: 1 pink snapdragon, 1 yellow protea, 1 orange protea, 2 yellow freesia stems, 1 medium 4" succulent, 1 pink peony)

1 block of floral foam

Thick green floral tape

2 to 3 very small plastic liners/ dishes (2" to 3" wide)

Optional: 1 to 2 pieces of 18"-long 20-gauge straight stem wire (if wiring succulents); reindeer or Spanish moss

Medium piece of grapewood

1 Soak the floral foam, then cut small 2" to 3" chunks of the foam and place them in the plastic dishes. Cut the foam so it's even with the top of the dishes. Wrap the floral tape over and around the foam and the dishes, crisscrossing as you go to keep the foam secure if it feels like it's going to fall out (see the Branch Out recipe on page 100).

2 Prep the flowers and cut them all to about 2" to 3" long. Put 3 flowers in each dish. The flowers should slightly hang over the dishes to conceal them as much as possible. You could also use reindeer or Spanish moss to cover the foam if you run out of flowers.

3 Lay out the grapewood wherever you want the arrangement, and place the plastic dishes next to the wood in openings between the branches. The flowers should rest on top of the wood so that they look like they're growing out of it. You can place the dishes next to each other, or on opposite sides of a branch. Try a few different placement options to see what you like best.

4 Remove the succulent from its container and clean off all the dirt, leaving just the small stem. Tuck it into a small crevice in the grapewood or just rest it on top of the grapewood.

the flower chef

ACKNOWLEDGMENTS

The best email I've ever received was from my now literary agent, Alyssa Reuben, who responded to my book proposal query with "you've piqued my interest." I knew it would take a young, smart woman to *get* what I was trying to do. Alyssa, words can never fully express my gratitude, but you know how much I love you and how forever grateful I am for you. Thank you for taking me on when I had very little to show, for the countless hours you invested, all of those edits, and for encouraging me to always do my best.

To Amanda Englander, you understood my vision from day one. Thank you for your belief and guidance! To Sara Weiss, thank you for organizing the book in a logical way—a huge turning point—and for the insight to bring Amara on board.

To Karen Murgolo and Morgan Hedden at Grand Central Life & Style and Jamie Raab at Hachette Book Group: Thank you for seeing this through to the end. I feel extremely blessed to have gotten to work with such a stellar publisher on my first book. Truly a dream come true!

Amara Holstein, you're my fairy godmother. That's all there is to it. I'm still amazed and in awe at how you took all of the offhand comments I made during the rewriting process and translated them into my voice. This book wouldn't be what it is without your thoughtful attention to detail. Thank you for the patience, time, and care that you put into this. I can only hope to work with you again!

Thank you to Lesley Bea for being the best cheerleader (and for cleaning up all the messes I made while experimenting in our apartment).

Thank you a million times to my dad, Larry, who was my first delivery driver. You're still my favorite person to set up an event with, and I cherish all of those crazy first weddings, first deliveries, and first events. I laugh in fondness thinking about driving your white van, working in the back of your store,

and texting you hours before an event in a frantic state asking you to pretty please come help us.

Thank you to my mom, Lauren, for always being supportive of every path I've taken. While my attempt to make pasta as a kid after watching Julia Child didn't lead me to becoming a real chef (thank you for washing my flour-dusted clothes that I tried to hide), it did lead me to become this kind of chef!

To my first client, Alle Fister, and the whole team at her communications firm, Bollare: You've been more than generous in your support. You inspire me to be classy in business and life, and to always pay it forward.

To all of the amazing designers who have ever worked with me over the years—I have surely learned more from each of you than you have from me. Special thanks to Caitlin Madden, Kristine Ota, Syretta Hatchett, Julia Osborne Ross, Rachel Keidan, and April Macias. Thanks to Nia Freshman, my "sous chef" on this book, and to Cristen Burrell, my "taste-tester" who convinced me to include a mason jar recipe.

To my entire family, and especially my brother, Matthew: Thank you for taking so many photos of my flowers (and me!) over the years. You're a good sport to put up with all my shenanigans. To my aunt, Adair (DD) Robbins, thank you for your honest feedback, unwavering support, and love of flowers.

A huge heartfelt thanks to my kind, kickass, intelligent girlfriends who have been there with me every step of the way over the last four years during this process: Lesley Bea, Kelly Bone, Cristen Burrell, Maureen Chase, Vanessa De Vargas, Whitney Galitz, Stephanie (Lester) Karpow, Nadiya Mazurczak, and Tina Tangalakis. Thank you to Caley (Lawson) Rinker, Noelle (Vazzano) Marchese, and Jami Templeton, who gave me all those little jobs starting out, which allowed me to hone my craft. To Kimberly Bragalone for those first wedding referrals—and for always doing my makeup flawlessly and making me look good! To Marion Coda for all of the badass graphic design. Thank you Sandy Abrams for navigating me through the entrepreneurial roads for which there's no road map.

I feel lucky to have had the most supportive, loving grandparents, and hope to emulate their character qualities I hold dear: Pop Bernie, your zest for life; Nana Peggy, your creative mind; Pop Joe, your calm demeanor; Grandma Dot, your keen eye. I love each of you, and keep you in my heart always. Lastly, thank you to Teri Lyn Fisher and Britni Wood. Your breathtaking photography and immaculate styling made my vision for this book a reality.

INDEX

Page numbers of photographs appear in italics.

ABOUT THE AUTHOR

CARLY CYLINDER started her floral design company in 2009 at twenty-six years old. What started as a daily delivery service based out of her small apartment quickly grew into a bicoastal, full-service design studio. She's worked with global brands as a spokesperson and creator of fresh DIY content across all platforms. She currently resides in Los Angeles.